My Brushes With Death And Other Outdoor Blunders

A Family Man's Guide To Hunting And Fishing Woe

By Steven Paul Barlow

Illustrations By David Harshberger

Published by Briar Hill Books, PO BOX 53, Homer, NY
13077

ISBN 978-0-9788704-0-9

All stories previously published by Game & Fish Publications
as indicated throughout.

Dedication

This book is dedicated to my wife Dawn, my children Matthew, Brian, Sean, and Stephanie, and to my brother Gary, all of whom by their outlandish behavior continue to be an inspiration to my writing. Thanks too for their reminders that I should laugh at myself every once in a while.

Contents

VI

Pulling Out The Duane

(Originally published by Game & Fish Publications, April 1992)

Of course I wouldn't mind bringing a complete stranger along. After all, I'd only been planning this outing for weeks, the trout were waiting for me and Duane had never fished before in his life.

My wife, Dawn, had invited an old college friend, Renee, up from the big city for a visit. A visit from Renee the Wretched was the best reason I could think of to go fishing. This time, though, Renee insisted on dragging along her most recent catch-of-the-day, Duane.

After Duane had carried in their luggage, there was nothing for him to do. The women didn't want him to stand around looking stupid while they talked about old times, so they decided Duane was going to be my weekend buddy.

Duane, Renee told us, was looking for a simple, mindless, stone-age hobby to occupy his free time. Renee said that when Duane had mentioned "stone-age", she immediately thought of me and how much I loved fishing.

Apparently Duane needed to relieve a little stress from his job as executive vice president for internal administrative affairs for some consultant firm's division of cost analysis.

"I hear you write about worms, flies, grubs and stinkbait?" Duane said. Everyone laughed. I smiled and secretly plotted to strangle Duane with ten-pound-test line.

It's amazing how we've managed to botch things up in only a few thousand short years, I thought. What was so

1

important about what a guy does for a living? It seems like only yesterday when man hunted and fished all day, every day instead of going to work, because back then there were no other jobs.

Then somewhere along the long line of human descent there was born a grotesque genetic aberration, a mutant life form born with a disdain for finding his own food.

While everyone else was content to be out hunting, fishing and whittling sticks, this creature, who probably looked like Duane, did little more than sit around and think about things, such as how to invent the wheel. A truly great mind would have invented the outboard motor first. Anyhow, once the wheel was invented, next came carts, wagons and things to put in them to be hauled around.

This mutant, in effect, created work where there had been none before. Honest fishermen were duped into performing such mundane tasks as toting firewood and hauling agricultural crops to market.

Free trade was established. People forgot how to hunt and fish, and moved into horrible places called cities. They learned specialized occupational tasks such as pushing buttons, shuffling papers and filing multiple copies.

If you're like Duane, one of those narrow, specialized occupations can fetch you a six-figure income. If you're like me, you can earn a six-figure income only if you include the two figures to the right of the decimal point.

In any case I was stuck teaching the art of fishing to Duane, the kind of guy whom I held personally responsible for inventing both the wheel and gainful employment.

"This should be great fun," Duane said as we rolled along in my pickup truck. "And this will give the girls some time to reminisce. Boy, it's hard to imagine now how wild Dawn was in college. Renee told me some stories and let me tell you..."

"Duane," I said calmly. "The stream where we're headed to has swift, swirling currents. The rocks are slippery. It wouldn't surprise anyone if a person suddenly fell in, smashed his head open on the rocks and sank to oblivion, never to be seen again." It was the only mature thing I could think to say. Why become hostile?

After that Duane chose his words carefully, which is to say that for the rest of the ride he chose not to speak at all. That changed when we reached the stream. Duane became inquisitive about everything. He was truly excited to be fishing and was intent on going about it the correct way.

"I've been reading up on this, but I still don't understand the difference between fishing and angling." There was concern in his voice.

"That's simple," I said after a moment's thought. "Fishing is the act of pursuing the fish. Angling has more to do with your stealthy approach to the stream. For a novice such as yourself I'd suggest a 45-degree angle."

Duane was all decked out in my waders, my fishing vest, my net and my creel. He bent to a back-breaking crouch and seriously inched his way toward the stream, my rod and reel in his hand. He looked like he was challenging the trout to a fencing duel.

"Perfect," I said. "You're a natural."

We performed the old bait and switch tactic all day, until we had exhausted every lure in the tackle box. Then we tried worms, grubs, minnows and egg sacks. The fish weren't biting. Duane sat down on the bank to rest.

"I've been thinking about this," he said.

"It's too late," I said. "The wheel's already been invented and we're both stuck with jobs. We're better off. We'd starve otherwise."

"No, I mean I've been thinking about the bait we've been using." He stood up, reached into his pocket and pulled out a ball of lint. Working quickly, he fashioned a crude fly on a hook. "If my calculations are correct..."

Duane waded into the stream and cast his invention

perfectly to a pool near the far bank. Instantly the water churned. The biggest trout I'd ever seen in that stream was choking on Duane's lint ball.

Duane fought a frantic battle against the trout and looked to be winning. He worked the trout closer, reached for the net, but suddenly slipped on a rock and fell out of sight into the pool. Deja vu.

I put all of my hostile feelings about Duane's six-figure income aside. In these dangerous currents I knew I had to act quickly to save my fishing gear. And there was still a glimmer of hope of landing the trout as well.

I dove into the water, lunged for Duane and pulled him ashore. The fish was gone. As we sat huddled and shivering on the shore, a smile came to Duane's face.

"You saved my life. Before in the truck I thought you were threatening me. But you were just warning this city kid of the dangers of the wild. I owe you my life."

"Oh, I don't know," I said, affecting a hero's modesty that I'd keep handy in case any television stations wanted to interview me later. "I suppose you could have drown in knee-deep water."

We stared off into the stream.

"Wow, what a fish, huh?" Duane said.

It was hard not to like a guy who was so impressed about losing a fish. Maybe Duane and I weren't so different after all. The more I thought about it, the more I realized that the day's endeavors at this trout stream had stripped our differences down to common denominators: to what we were centuries ago and to what we are still deep inside.

"I'd like to try this again," Duane said.

"It's too bad Renee switches boyfriends so often," I said. "Otherwise we'd love to have you the next time she comes to visit."

F.O.R.T.Y., F.A.T. A.N.D. F.O.O.L.I.S.H.

(Originally published in Game & Fish Publications, October 1991)

Are you in shape for the long hunting seasons ahead? If the first thing to go on an outdoorsman is his physique, the last thing to come is his willingness to admit it.

I guess I've always assumed that when I became a hunter a certain amount of ruggedness was supplied with it. And for me the word 'rugged' conjures up images of a tough outdoorsman, hardened from countless treks into the remotest regions, skilled in the ways of the wild, able to live off the land and make his way through the harshest circumstances alone and unwavering by his wits and brute strength.

"You, rugged?" My wife, Dawn, chuckled. "I've seen you after those hunting trips. For you rugged is just a polite way of saying that you haven't bathed recently. Scruffy is a better word. You're no mountain man, especially since you've gained so much weight."

I was so mad I almost sat up on the sofa. Maybe I had gained weight. But I was still rugged, in my sense of the word, not hers. So I had to accept the challenge when she bet that she could lose ten pounds before I could.

I grabbed pencil and paper. I wasn't going to panic and submit to needless, random exercise without a plan.

Ten minutes later Dawn was on her way out the door.

"I'm going to jog down to my aerobics lesson now," she said. "Then I'm going to pick up some watercress for my

dinner. I put a double batch of fudge brownies in the oven for you. They'll be done in 15 minutes."

What a rotten tactic. Still there wasn't much I could do in 15 minutes so I decided to rest my eyes for a minute.

What a nightmare! There I was enrolled in a hunter fitness and rehabilitation camp. I sat in a classroom filled with paunchy middle-aged men in red hunter's plaid.

"F.O.R.T.Y., F.A.T. A.N.D. F.O.O.L.I.S.H." the instructor spelled out. "That's why you're in this camp. It stands for 'Facetiously Obtaining Ruggedness Through Yearly Fitness And Training All Nicely Developed For Overweight Outdoorsmen Like I See Here.'"

The final exam in this hunter fitness camp was a grueling obstacle course designed to test the limits of physical conditioning and hunting proficiency.

On this obstacle course I found myself swatting swarms of malaria-plagued mosquitoes as I clung by my teeth to a vine overhanging a pool infested with man-eating alligators.

Then, suddenly, my life was saved. The oven buzzer sounded, my brownies were done. I awoke drenched in sweat, sure that I lost all ten pounds in that short 15 minutes.

But more important, I now had some great ideas for a fitness plan for outdoorsmen. I had the entire plan on paper before I had finished two-thirds of the brownies.

The key was to design activities that both improve hunting skills and condition the body. And if you're like me -- heaven help you -- you persevere several hunting seasons each year and need an exercise plan for each one.

For woodchuck hunters I've designed a range much like a golf course with one steel woodchuck target outside each of the 18 holes. If you miss, the woodchuck dives into the hole, pops back up and sticks his tongue out at you. You must carry your own rifle; no caddies allowed.

For grouse hunters I've designed a two-player competition where the hunters take turns springing out of the brush scaring the heck out of each other to simulate flushing birds. For safety reasons no loaded guns are allowed on this course.

For the ultimate test in hunter ruggedness I've designed a day-long, iron-man competition.

It's difficult from the start. After having stayed up until 2 a.m. talking strategy, you have to get up before daylight, make your way to a closet filled with the acquisitions of 100 garage sales and there, in the dark, find all the hunting equipment you placed there exactly one year ago and haven't seen since.

From there you move outside, start a pickup truck, and while you hold one foot on the accelerator so it won't stall out, you have to reach out and scrape a peep hole through the frost on the windshield.

Then, as you drive to the next phase of the course over a pitted dirt road, you have to pour scalding hot coffee, drink two cups down instantly and dump a third in your lap.

At the second phase you park the truck up to the axles in a mud hole. You step out of the truck, throw the keys on the seat and lock the doors.

Then you jog across a cornfield, tripping through the stubble until you reach a wooded area, somewhere in which is a tree stand with every other rung on the ladder broken.

When you get to the top you have to sit there for three hours in blizzard conditions without twitching. Then you scan the woods with binoculars -- they're provided; let's not make it too tough -- until you spot camouflaged sandbags weighing 200 lbs, simulating a downed deer.

Then, in a crouched position, you must drag the sandbags for three miles through tangled brush, over logs and across streams to the Phase Three checkpoint.

The clock starts on Phase Three when you hug a wet retriever, jump into a boat and row 200 yards to where you must pluck a dozen duck decoys out of the water. One is motorized and under remote control by competition officials.

After you retrieve the last decoy you dive into the water to simulate falling overboard. You swim back to the boat, which is now 50 yards away in a strong current.

Back on shore, you gather one bushel of sticks and start a fire using a dewdrop as a magnifying lens. After digging edible roots and tubers for your lunch, you're ready for Phase Four.

You unleash a brace of undisciplined beagles into an endless tract of pricker bushes, then try to catch them after they've run off in separate directions.

Phase Five is the skill portion of the competition. Clay pigeons are launched behind you. You must turn, select one of five shotguns, four of which have empty chambers.

If you select one of the wrong shotguns you must fumble through the 20 pockets of your jacket until you find a shell that fits the gun. Then you must hit the bird, no alibis accepted.

For the final phase, you must find your way out of a swamp before nightfall equipped only with a street map of Los Angeles. Failing this, you must build a lean-to, snare a rabbit and spend the night in the woods listening to the recorded cries of hungry carnivorous wildlife.

Winners will be officially designated as "rugged".

Losers must find a way into their locked pickup trucks and pull them out of the mud. As a consolation prize they can redeem their hunting licenses for a viewer's guide to weekend football telecasts.

Will I compete in these events myself? Of course not. I would have an unfair advantage because I invented the program. But with all of this talk about exercise, I've worked up quite an appetite. I think I'll concede the bet and get some milk to go with the rest of these brownies.

Bring Extras
Just In Case

(Originally published by Game & Fish Publications, November 1995)

I was preparing for my annual week-long wilderness deer hunt and I had just dumped the contents of my old trunk into a jumbled heap on the floor.

My youngest son, Sean, obviously attracted by the sound of things breaking, walked into the room to see if he could join in the fun.

"What are you playing, Dad?" he asked.

"I'm playing 'Getting Ready To Go Hunting'," I said.

"Can I play," he asked.

"Well, I guess you can help," I said. "You see I'm sorting all of my equipment, deciding what to bring on my hunting trip."

This sorting of equipment had become a pre-hunt ritual. I almost always packed the same equipment, and almost always left the same things home. But the process conjured up pleasant memories of past hunts and helped to soothe the restless anticipation I felt for the upcoming trip.

"What's this?" Sean asked.

"That's a water filter," I said. "We used to have to carry a ton of water with us to cook all of those lightweight instant foods. Now, if there's a stream nearby, we can pump out all of the water we need once we get there.

"The only problem is that the place where we usually camp is a long way from the nearest stream. So, instead of

10

hunting, I end up spending more time lugging the heavy water jugs from the stream to camp."

"Is that why Mom says you never catch a deer?"

"Mom was joking. Look, you put this hose in the water and this hose in your empty water jug. All of the little bugs in the water that can make you sick get trapped in the filter, so only clean water goes into the jug."

"Are the bugs still in the filter?"

"I don't know. I suppose so. I'm sure they're all dead by now."

"Can I see them?"

"No. They're too small to see."

"I caught some bugs once, but they died too. I still have them in my room. Do you want me to go get them?"

"No. You can show them to Mom later."

"Mom doesn't like bugs."

"Mom was only joking," I said. "I'm sure she'd love to see them."

"What's this?"

"That's a compass. You hold it level and the needle always points north. Over there is east, that's south and west is that way. You check the compass every so often while you're hunting so you can keep track of which direction you're going so you won't get lost."

"Are you going to get lost again this time?"

"What do you mean 'again'?"

"Mon says we should get a new dog if you get lost again, one that can smell your blood."

"You mean a bloodhound? I think Mom was exaggerating."

"Is that kind of like joking?"

"Kind of."

"But I heard her tell you to get lost when you asked her for money to buy more bullets. So I think it's okay with Mom if I get a new dog."

"We're not going to get a new dog and I'm not going to get

lost. See, I even carry an extra compass just in case."

"Do you bring two of everything just in case?"

"Only just in case Uncle Gary's going along. He tends to forget lots of things."

"Did you ever forget your bullets?"

"No. See, I have this handy cartridge carrier that fits right on my belt."

"How many bullets do you need?"

"Usually I only need one or two."

"Then how come you told Mom you needed more?"

"We're going to be up there for a week. I need more just in case I see a deer and I miss."

"I wouldn't miss if I went hunting. Mom says you wouldn't always want to buy new guns if you'd learn how to shoot the old ones. How many guns are you going to bring?"

"Just one."

"Aren't you going to bring an extra just in case?"

"No. That would be too much to carry."

"What if you get lost because one compass breaks and the other one you gave to Uncle Gary because he forgot his?"

"I'd fire my gun to signal to the other hunters."

"But what if you ran out of bullets because Mom wouldn't let you buy more and you didn't bring an extra gun because it was too heavy?"

"Well, then I'd have to live off of the land until I found my way out."

"Grandma and Grandpa say you live off of Mom because you write about hunting instead of going to work like most dads. They said I was going to have a doctor for my dad, but then Mom met you."

"Grandma and Grandpa were joking too."

"Grandma and Grandpa are coming to visit, aren't they?"

"Yes, how did you know?"

"Mom says every time Grandma and Grandpa come to visit you go hunting."

"Silly old Mom."

"What's this orange thing?"

"That's a nylon tarp. We set that up in our camp and we can spot it from far away. At the end of the day we meet back at camp. It's usually raining or snowing by then. So we all sit on a log under the tarp, cook our instant, powdered dinners, stare out at the rain and the darkness, and grumble about not seeing any deer all day. It's fun."

"I hope I can have fun like that some day."

"I'm sure you will."

"Mom says she thinks I'm going to be a doctor."

"You can still go hunting even if you become a doctor."

"Awesome. And if you get lost can I get a new dog?"

"If I get lost, then you can ask Grandma and Grandpa to buy you a new dog. Maybe they can find one that can track down a doctor."

Kindergarten, Patience, And Fly Fishing

(Originally published by Game & Fish Publications, April 1994)

My attempts at learning how to fish with a fly rod have merely reinforced in my mind that I am not a patient person.

It wasn't always so. As a child I could sit for hours in naive bliss with paper and crayons, scribbling dogs and bunny rabbits until I had drawn them perfectly.

It wasn't until kindergarten, when a fellow student of the arts pointed out that my dogs didn't look like dogs and my bunnies didn't look like bunnies, that I became more frustrated, self-critical, and therefore less patient.

Perhaps, she said, if I could have drawn the proper number of legs and tails and ears and things it might have made a difference, although that had never stopped Picasso.

At that stage of my development I learned that I was much more talented at tearing up those pictures, throwing blocks at my fellow student of the arts and standing in the corner while everyone else went to recess.

And so it continued until the day, half of a lifetime later, when I decided I'd take up fly fishing. Now I had been a fisherman for years. After all, anyone could crank a bunch of hardware through the water. But to gracefully wave a fly rod to gently present a fly to a trout was like a painter stroking a brush on canvas. It was raising sport to the level of art.

I was in for an experience many times more grueling than kindergarten. The first thing I learned is that the equipment is a little more complicated.

In the past, I could go to a department store and buy a rod and reel combo all set to go. Decisions were easy. I could choose a light action rig with six-pound test line if I intended just to snag on lilly pads or a heavier outfit with 10- or 15-pound test for submerged logs and discarded tires.

As a novice fly fisherman, choices were harder. Most of the reading I'd done advised to buy the best equipment I could afford. Nonsense. I couldn't afford any of it. That's why I wanted to go fishing in the first place: to forget for short periods of time how much of everything in this world I could not afford.

Everyone suggested a different length rod, from the standard pole vault length to the popular hook and ladder variety, all with the heftiness of a willow sprig. The reels seemed deceptively simple because they seemed to perform no function except to store the line.

And the line wasn't just line. First you reeled on this thick, braided dental floss-looking stuff called backing. Then came the line itself that looked like coated telephone wire. It not only came in different weights, but different configurations as well: level, double-taper, weight-forward, floating, sinking, and on and on.

After the backing and the line, you had to attach the monofilament leader, usually tapered on one end. The leaders came in different diameters and were designated by a secret code, such as: 2X, 3X and 4X.

The last leg of the journey to the actual fly was the tippet material, which after handling the heavy line, seemed as fine as if I had pulled out a hair and was trying to tie a lure to it. If I wasn't already balding, I probably would have pulled out quite a few hairs at this point.

The key, my friends told me, was that the entire system of

rod, reel, line, leader, etc. had to be matched. Otherwise I might as well go back to throwing blocks.

Once I had all of the basic equipment purchased on credit, I had to assemble it. That meant tying knots. Now if I had spent more time with the crayons in kindergarten I might have developed more manual dexterity than it takes to slap a mosquito on the back of my neck.

When it came to knot-tying expertise, I had been graduated no further than the half hitch. If a more sturdy knot was required, I would throw on a few more half hitches. Undoing a grapefruit-sized ball of half hitches, I found with my usual patience, was no harder than opening a blade on a pocket knife.

With fly fishing, a different knot was now required for each connection: backing to reel, line to backing, leader to line, tippet to leader and fly to tippet.

The first, a modified slip knot, I modified by using a couple of half hitches, which slipped on me most of the time anyway so it wouldn't be a problem. Then I ran into problems. The knot diagrams were confusing.

I took one look at the needle knot and opted to go with the nail knot, which wouldn't hold no matter how hard I hammered. I drew blood on the blood knot, the cinch knot wasn't, I was too slow on the turtle, and I could have completed medical school before learning to tie the double surgeon.

My wife, Dawn, who has no understanding of male pride, suggested that I ask another fisherman how to tie the knots. That would be like meeting another hunter in the woods and asking him how to load my shotgun, I told her.

She told me to stop acting like I was in kindergarten. I told her that when I was in kindergarten I never hesitated to ask for help. Why, I had even asked my teacher, Miss Applecore to tie my sneakers one day.

I already knew how to tie my sneakers, of course, but I

needed them laced tightly that day to outrun a certain third-grade bully, who just so happened to have an artsy little sister in kindergarten.

In my second year of fly fishing, after having assembled my components as best I could manage, it was time to learn to cast.

The first part was easy. I walked into my backyard and stripped the line from my reel until I had gobs of it lying in a tangled mess at my feet. This, I thought, wasn't any different than fishing with a baitcasting reel.

I yanked the leader-line connection through the guides without to much trouble. The knotted mass would be more streamlined, I supposed, if I had had the patience to file down the nail that I had never gotten out of my nail knot.

Casting was great fun. I swung the rod hither and yon and remembered to duck when the line whipped back toward my face. I recalled the time as a five-year-old apprentice cowboy when I had cut a section of my mom's clothesline to use as a bullwhip and then as a lasso to snare the neighbor's dog.

I never caught the neighbor's dog. Now much more adroit as an adult with a fly rod, I was cracking the line like a bullwhip and then managed to lasso the only obstacle in my backyard: a branch of a maple tree 30 feet off the ground.

My neighbor, Lenny, must have been watching the show from his window. He came outside carrying a chainsaw the moment I had tangled my line in the tree. Lenny had been after me to get rid of the tree because some of the branches hung over into his yard and scraped against his bedroom window.

Now, faced with the alternative of having to cut my line and tie another nail knot, I nodded my consent and let Lenny kill my tree.

In my third year of fly fishing I was actually ready to fish a stream. Dawn had delegated to me the job of watching our five-year-old son, Sean, for the day. We headed to a shallow limestone creek not far from our house.

Since it was the middle of the week, we had the place to ourselves until I set up my fly rod. Then dozens of people filtered in to watch me embarrass myself. Sean walked upstream to discover new species of crawling, biting creatures.

One word of caution to other novice fly fishermen. Because the fly rod is so long, you have to break yourself of the tendency to swing the rod around with you when you turn your head to look at something.

What, would you suppose, are the odds of turning around and inadvertently swatting a young woman right on the insignia of her designer jeans? One in a million, right? I said as much to her boyfriend, whose sport was obviously football and not fly fishing.

I walked up and down the stream for a few minutes, waded in and out of the water, and rubbed my chin in the most pensive attitude I could affect. When I thought I had appeared knowledgeable enough to the onlookers, I opened a small box of flies.

The one I chose, I think, was the Royal Caddis, Short-hackled, Minnow Muddler Coachman, Wooly Wulff Stonefly Nymph. The Latin name escapes me. It was one of those little brown, fuzzy thingies.

I bent over and made a stealthy approach to the stream. It was then that Sean came splashing downstream shouting that he had caught a crayfish.

He begged me to let him keep it. I reluctantly agreed and he placed the critter in my otherwise empty creel. I then pointed out, as dads are supposed to do, that his sneakers were sopping wet and untied.

Sean sat down, grabbed the wet laces and hurriedly tied a couple of half hitches. He couldn't wait, he said, to show Mom what he captured.

Maybe I'll have to wait until my fourth or fifth year of fly fishing before I actually catch a fish. I don't know if I'll have the patience to wait that long. Maybe I should have started when I was in kindergarten.

The Flavor Of Lures, The Lure Of Money

(Originally published in Game & Fish Publications, August 1991)

Can you keep a secret? My brother-in-law, whom I shall call Floyd because that's his name and this is a family magazine and I can't mention what I usually call him, just approached me with one of his sure-fire, can't-miss investment opportunities. I thought I'd pass it along to you.

Now before you start sending in those hefty checks or money orders (Floyd changes addresses frequently and prefers cash), I suppose I should be at least partially truthful with you about some of Floyd's unusual get-rich-quick schemes.

For instance, I'll never forgive him for the time he talked me into that charter fishing boat venture. Floyd's Economy Chartered Fishing Tours we called it. We were supposed to be partners, 50-50, but I ended up doing all the rowing.

Then there was the time he was going to make deer grunt calls from recycled car radiator hoses. Floyd borrowed a hose and experimented with the calls for a whole afternoon until every dairy cow within five miles was lounging in my front yard listening to Floyd's concert.

I thought my wife, Dawn, would be more upset, but I think she was too exhausted after her ten-mile hike home when her car mysteriously overheated.

This time it's a whole new concept in fishing lures.

"Try one," said Floyd. He handed me a brown rubber worm. "They're edible."

21

"You've got to be kidding?"

"No look," he said and popped one into his mouth. "They're really intended to attract fish, but people will love them too. Flavor lasts longer than chewing gum. Sugar-free, too."

I reluctantly took the bait. "Ugh, this tastes like..."

"Like roast beef, right?"

I couldn't answer. My gag reflex had kicked in.

"Well, okay," he said. "It needs a little work, maybe a little investment capital."

We walked into my house after deciding to discuss the idea further over a bottle of syrup of ipecac.

"Flavored fishing lures isn't a bad idea," I said. "There are all kinds of fish attractants on the market now. But shouldn't you go with something that's designed to please the fish? You know, worm flavored worms, crayfish flavored crayfish, grasshopper flavored grasshoppers?"

"How do we know what flavors fish would really prefer if given more of a variety?" said Floyd as he probed my kitchen cupboards. "I mean maybe they'd never look at another worm if they could eat donuts to their hearts' content. Have any milk to go with these?"

"I see. You mean let them eat cake?"

"I mean it's just like your mother used to tell you: 'How do you know you don't like asparagus if you've never tried it.'"

"I hate asparagus."

"Okay, we'll do without the asparagus. But think of all the other flavors in the world. There must be some that are irresistible to both fish and man. When we find them they'll sell like hotcakes. Hey, there's another flavor to try."

Floyd had a convincing argument. He pointed out that manufacturers have experimented for years with different lure actions and colors. Sometimes they started with what looked and moved naturally, but more often found the most effective ones resemble nothing found in nature.

"When was the last time," Floyd pointed out, "that you came across a real, live worm with a purple head, chartreuse tail and red metallic speckles throughout? But they work. And just as important, they attract the eyes of as many fishermen as fish. So they sell. Maybe we could do the same with flavors.

"And flashy lures, like flashy neckties, are always in and out of style so you have to keep buying more. I have this theory that fashion trends in neckties follow the colors and patterns in popular fishing lures. The difference is that you're always given more ties than you can use and never enough fishing lures. You always lose fishing lures, but somehow can never lose those flashy ties.

"And another thing. Why do you suppose food manufacturers put such taste-tempting photos on product packaging?" he said. We were in my den now and Floyd rummaged through the drawers in my desk. "Appetites that's why. Where do you keep your checkbook? You always buy more at the grocery store when you're hungry, right?"

"Yeah, so what?"

"Have you no vision? Don't you think customers in tackle shops get hungry?"

"Wait a minute," I said. "We tried that concept with Floyd's Shoreline Bait and Pizza Shop remember? And the health department shut us down because you got caught putting salted minnows on the pizzas instead of anchovies."

"This is different, more sublime. We'll supply other shops with the lures. And we'll have a warning on the label not to eat them after you attach the hooks. Pizza. Not a bad idea. I'll bet if you baited a hook with a piece of pepperoni you'd get a strike instantly. We can create a rubber worm that tastes just like the pizzas we used to make."

"That's easy. All we need is a few pieces of soggy

cardboard."

"Be serious," he said. "We've only got a half hour before the bank closes. You want to give me gas money or should we take your car?"

Just a few weeks later, there we were on Little Stump Lake.

"Row a little faster, will you," said Floyd, "I want to get closer to those weed beds." We experimented with our new flavored worms all morning.

"Pass the baked beans, please," Floyd said. "Thank you. More mashed potatoes?"

"No thanks," I said, "but I think I got a nibble on the turkey and stuffing a minute ago. Have you tried the chicken wings yet?"

"The bass like the hot ones, but I think we'll have to go mild for perch."

"What flavor are these?" I said and held up a Styrofoam cup. "They're not labeled." I scooped a couple into my mouth.

"I don't believe it." Floyd stared in amazement. "You just ate my control group. Every scientific experiment has to have a control group."

"Control group? What are you talking about?" I said. "They taste kind of like chocolate pudding, but with a funny aftertaste. Got potential, though."

Floyd picked up the oars for the first time in his life and started rowing like a madman for shore.

"What are you doing?" I asked.

"I want to get on firm ground so I can run like heck."

"Run?"

"Yeah. I know you're gonna be mad when you realize you just ate live nightcrawlers."

Deer John
And Veniston Stu

(Originally published in Game & Fish Publications, November 1991)

Deer season is a great motivator. The advent of deer season turns otherwise lifeless, miserable grown men into spirited adolescents, known collectively as a sportsmen's club.

In the worst throes of their malignancy, these club members are willing to wake up early, chop wood, sweep floors, repair roofs, cook, wash dishes and eagerly do all manner of things they would never do around their own homes, all in the name of camaraderie and the thrill of the hunt.

The Little Stump Lake Hunting and Fishing Club was founded several years ago by such a motivated group of sportsmen who confronted the hapless Leo A. Minuscule about forming the organization.

Minuscule was a social misfit until the day he was voted in as President-for-Life of the club. That was the same day he donated to the club his entire inheritance: his family homestead on Little Stump Lake that consisted of about fifty acres of gone-to-seed farmland, but included lake frontage and adjoined about a thousand acres of very hunt-able state forest land.

Leo wasn't a hunter or a fisherman, didn't know buck from bass, but took great pride in taking gavel in hand to preside over the club's monthly meetings that included all the members of the executive committee.

There was Ed "Mr. Big Bucks" Finicky, the town banker,

and club treasurer, who always talked with interest about the big bucks he'd seen, though we all knew his only experiences were with a lot of doe.

There was John Bachelor, the club secretary, whom we called "Deer John" because his wife left him a note on club stationery one day saying that she was fed up with him taking off on hunting trips all the time and how she had found a new life with the town undertaker.

Lawrence Smartdresser was the club's resident lawyer. "Loophole Larry" as we called him could talk a good case about things that needed to be done around camp, but always seemed to find a way out of doing any chores himself.

Stuart Grizzle or "Venison Stu" as we called him, was the rather absent-minded camp cook who always seemed to stir up a lot of controversy.

It was Venison Stu who started all the commotion the evening before one deer season opener when he offered a little side bet on the club's annual big buck contest.

Deer John was the perennial favorite to win the contest. He was the best marksman in the club and the most patient hunter. Most of the trophy racks that graced the walls of the Leo A. Minuscule Memorial Clubhouse had been taken by him.

That's why everyone thought Venison Stu was crazy when he offered even money that Leo A. Minuscule himself would take the biggest buck on opening day.

It was more surprising when you considered that Deer John and Venison Stu were good friends. And Stu prided himself on the fact that he provided all the handloaded rifle cartridges John had used to win so many competitions.

Members of the executive committee were split on the debate. Some argued that to take a great buck the odds favored a skilled hunter such as Deer John.

Venison Stu and others insisted that mere chance had more to do with it and that if Leo was in the right place at the right time, even he could tag a trophy.

The gentlemen continued their discussion in the usual sporting tradition with property damage and the loss of dignity kept to a minimum. Then there came a soft tap, tap, tap from the head of the table.

Leo A. "President for Life" Minuscule was trying to restore order to the meeting. When he had summoned the courage to speak, he said he enjoyed discussions on the classic philosophical questions as applied to deer hunting.

However, the idea of resolving those great ponderances through a display of his yet untested outdoor skills was enough to make him break out in hives, especially when the destiny of a great deal of money depended on his performance.

He reminded us that he had never hunted a day in his life, although he did possess the obligatory valid hunting license, purchased as a formality, something his stature as club president demanded.

Loophole Larry was quick to counter that the terms of the wager had already been established, the money was on the table and the entire business arrangement had been consummated with handshakes all around.

There was substantial case law in these matters, according to Loophole, and any willful reneging by either side would leave Leo, as president of the organization, subject to a nasty lawsuit, if not criminal prosecution.

So Leo spent the few remaining hours before dawn huddled in conference with Venison Stu, inundated with myths on firearms, wildlife biology, scrapes, rubs, scents, grunt calls, tracking techniques, and Boone and Crockett criteria.

All opening day, as hunter met hunter in the woods, everyone asked for progress reports on the contestants.

Rumor had it that Deer John had shot a buck at first light and speculation increased the size of that deer with each passing hour.

But at the end of the day it was a deerless John who trudged into camp muttering something about it being impossible to hunt when everybody kept coming up to him asking, "Got one yet?"

There had been no confirmed sightings of Venison Stu or his protege, Leo, since they had set out that morning. By 10 p.m. everyone was sure they were either lost, dead or ashamed to come back.

But a little while later a state police car pulled up outside the clubhouse and out of the back popped Venison Stu and Leo, both smiling, their clothes in tatters.

"We win!" shouted Venison Stu. "Leo dropped a four-pointer. Not really big, but a winner."

"Where is it?" asked Deer John.

"Down at Murphy's Towing," said Leo. "The deer ran in front of my pickup truck. My first deer and I didn't fire a shot. Truck's a total loss, though."

After another lengthy debate, the bet was declared a draw because the manner in which Leo had taken the deer was deemed outside the bounds of club protocol.

It was also discovered that the absent-minded Venison Stu had neglected to put gun powder in the last batch of cartridges he loaded for Deer John. Whether or not he knew about it at the time of the wager became the new hot topic of debate at the club.

Because Leo did acquire his deer accidentally, it did show that sometimes luck can be a bigger advantage than skill.

For that reason both sides voted to spend the wager money to mount Leo's trophy in the club's most coveted location. To this very day, members of the Little Stump Lake Hunting and Fishing Club can look with wonder above the fireplace mantel at the bumper, grille and one headlight from Leo A. Minuscule's pickup truck.

How To Find The Time

(Originally published by Game & Fish Publications, August 1996)

My wife, Dawn, stood in the doorway to the bathroom, her hands on her hips, demanding to know what I was doing.

"You're supposed to be giving Stephanie a bath," she said. "What's with all of the fishing rods?"

"We're fishing for the soap," I said. "Okay, Stephanie, cast over the structure formed by the boats we sank earlier. That's a girl, right between the rubber duck and that patch of bubbles. Hey, no splashing."

"For Pete's sake, she's not even a year old," Dawn scolded.

"She's got to learn sooner or later. I had to give her a bath anyway, so I figured I'd teach her how to fish at the same time. When she gets older maybe she'll beg me to go fishing and I'll get extra time on the water."

I know, I know. You've said the same thing a thousand times yourself. You'd love to do more hunting, fishing, shooting, camping, hiking, canoeing and general outdoor knocking about if only you could find the time.

The trouble is there will never be more than 24 hours in a day. The depressing truth, therefore, is that you will never have more time than you have right now.

Since you'll never have more time, there are two things you can do with the time you've got. First, you can rearrange your priorities and eliminate all of the unnecessary activities that are taking time away from your outdoor pursuits.

The second thing you can do is make more efficient use of

your time by streamlining or combining tasks, such as giving your daughter a bath and teaching her to fish at the same time.

Start by making two lists: a "must-do" list and a "want-to" list. On the "must-do" list include all of the things that are absolutely crucial to your survival, such as working for a living, and driving your mother-in-law to bingo night. On your "want-to" list include hunting, fishing and all of the other fun things you'd do if you had the time.

"This is incredible," I said as I showed my lists to Dawn. "I'm not greedy. All I'm asking for is one day a week to hunt, fish or hike, and maybe another couple of hours a week to shoot at the range. On paper I should have loads of free time. I work 40 to 50 hours a week. Where does the rest of the time go?"

"Well," Dawn said, "you've got your work hours listed, but not the time it takes you to get ready in the morning or make the commute. You didn't list picking the kids up from after-school activities, helping them with their homework or taking them to soccer games on the weekend.

"What about the time you spend sitting in front of the television or in the bathroom reading?" she continued. "And I still want to talk to you about mowing the lawn, painting the house and, oh yes, the sink's leaking worse now than before you fixed it."

I recalculated my figures and found that the tasks on my "must-do" list added up to 23 1/2 hours a day, seven days a week.

"Now I just have to decide whether I want to use that 1/2-hour of free time a day to hunt and fish or to eat and sleep."

I began to realize that I wasn't really wasting time, but that I was losing time in the translation between "real time", "outdoor time" and "wife's time."

"Real time" is made up of the seconds, minutes, hours and days that we normally use to measure time. Never use "real time" if you want to set aside any activities for yourself.

Instead, use "outdoor time." "Outdoor time" is measured in activities, not minutes and hours. You've used "outdoor time" on many occasions probably without realizing it.

Say you've been out fishing most of the day and your stomach, not your watch, tells you it's getting close to dinner time. You say to yourself, "Just three more casts and I'll head for home." Notice you didn't say, "Just five more minutes and I'll head for home." That would be "real time."

"Three more casts" is activity-oriented, it's "outdoor time" and it could translate to five minutes or five hours of "real time", depending on whether or not you start catching fish on those three casts.

The "one day a week to hunt, fish or hike" that I put on my "want-to" list could actually translate to a full week of "real time" if you factor in all of the planning and shopping for new equipment and supplies before the activity and the cool-down period at the diner afterwards.

Wives, in general, and Dawn, in particular, don't understand "outdoor time". If you say you're going hunting, most likely your wife will ask you what time you'll be home. If you reply, "I don't know," she's apt to get mad.

She wouldn't understand that you really don't know. If you get cold or bored or hungry you could be home in a couple of hours. If you get on the fresh track of a big buck, it'll be well after dark by the time you get home.

To make matters worse, wives in general and Dawn in particular don't understand "real time" either. Wives deal exclusively in "wife's time."

"Wife's time" is activity-oriented too, but is always measured in one-minute intervals.

Dawn will always summon me to a major household project by saying, "Can you come here for a minute? I want your opinion on this new wallpaper for the baby's room." Even worse is, "Can you take a minute before you go fishing to help me move a couple of things in the living room?"

31

You could protest and try to explain that by the time you translate from "outdoor time" to "wife's time" to "real time" you just won't have the time.

That won't work. Your wife will mostly likely say, "But you go fishing all of the time."

Now isn't that an interesting idea?

Compatible

(Originally published by Game & Fish Publications, March 1999)

To get the most enjoyment from the outdoors, you must continually confront issues of compatibility.

Compatibility problems could arise, for instance, if while hunting you discover your 12 gauge shotshells, the only ammo you brought, will not chamber in your .22 rifle, the only gun you brought.

If you discover on the lake that there might be a compatibility problem between your 50-pound canoe and your 350-pound fishing buddy, your enjoyment of the outing could be in jeopardy, unless, of course, you enjoy swimming to shore.

Many compatibility issues arise from equipment problems. I needed a new rifle scope, and found a good one at a great price. But when I got home, I found the beautiful, new scope was somehow not compatible with my battered, old rifle.

This problem was easy to solve. I simply bought a new rifle to go with the new scope. My wife, Dawn, disagreed with my solution, which, she said, was indicative of a much larger compatibility problem.

If you hunt with a dog, it's not so much how compatible you are as how much you're willing to tolerate.

Riding in the front seat? I can tolerate that. Nose-shaped smudges on the windows, barking at passing cars, wagging a tail in my face as he sticks his head out of the passenger window? No problem.

Flushing a family of skunks? Retrieving the decoy instead

of the duck? Finding and eating something long dead, getting carsick on the ride home, then biting me when I try to give him a bath? Sorry, not compatible.

The biggest compatibility concerns, of course, involve your hunting and fishing partners.

You can avoid the situation altogether by hunting and fishing alone. But then there's no one to share the adventure -- no one to help you land the fish, drag the deer or fill the gas tank on the way home when you suddenly can't find your wallet.

When you go it alone, you still do just as much talking, but it's to yourself and objects around you.

"Boy, it's a beautiful day," you say to yourself. "Okay, nice and easy now, right about here," you say to your boat.

"Let's see, you look like a nice one," you say as you select a worm. "All right, let's catch a big one," you tell your rod and reel. "Nice cast," you congratulate yourself.

"Got one!" you shout to them all. "Come on, Baby, just a little bit more. Oh, no, you son of a pup!" you say to the fish. "Look at that," again to yourself. "Snapped the line."

Talking to things shouldn't worry you until those things start talking back and someone you pass tells you later that he overheard both sides of the conversation.

A compatible fishing partner is someone who likes to start and stop fishing at about the same hours of the day as you, who doesn't complain about how many chili dogs you ate for lunch, and who never says, "Ha, ha, I caught more fish than you," even though he might think it.

For a compatible hunting partner I have Dave. Dave and I think alike. Take last fall's deer hunt for instance. After hunting all day, Dave and I were supposed to rendezvous at the clearing between the thicket and the hardwoods about an hour before dark.

I waited there for a half hour, but no Dave. "I'll bet he went back to the truck." After years of hunting alone, naturally, I said this aloud.

I went back to the truck and still no Dave. It was Dave's truck and I didn't have a key. "No need to worry," I said. "Dave can take care of himself."

"Who are you talking to?" Mike and Pete had pulled up in their truck and had overheard my conversation. "Any luck?" they asked.

"Nothing," I said. "I'm just waiting for Dave. He ought to be here any minute." Mike and Pete drove off.

Then I heard a shot. "That had to be Dave," I said. "I'll bet he got turned around in the thick stuff."

I fired a shot in return to help Dave get his bearings back to the truck. All was quiet for a long time.

"You know," I said, "maybe Dave was waiting at the other clearing, the one between the thicket and the corn field. Now that he's heard my shot and knows I'm waiting for him back at the truck, he'll probably be on his way back along the north trail."

I decided to start up the north trail to meet him. Dave, meanwhile, got tired of waiting for me at the clearing between the thicket and the corn field. "I'll bet that goof went to the wrong clearing," he said. Dave talks to himself, too.

Dave cut through the thicket to the other clearing, where I had been an hour earlier. He saw a six-pointer and shot it. When he heard my return shot, he said, "Good, he knows I got one and is on his way to help me drag it. I'll start down the south trail with it."

Dave dragged the deer all the way back to his truck by himself. He saw my footprints and the tire tracks from Mike's truck in the snow.

"He must have gotten a ride with Mike and Pete," he said. "He probably fired that signal shot to let me know he was out of the woods. I'll give him a call when I get home." Dave drove home.

Meanwhile, I had hiked all the way up the north trail to the clearing between the thicket and the corn field and no Dave. I whistled. No response. All was quiet, and dark, very dark.

"Hey, Dave!" I shouted to Dave, but it might as well have been to myself since Dave was miles away in his truck by then.

As I thought about it all night in the woods, I was convinced that Dave and I really do think alike. You see, the year before nearly the same thing happened when I left Dave stranded in the woods. If we weren't so compatible, I might suspect this time he did it on purpose.

You Gotta Eat It

(Originally published by Game & Fish Publications, July 2004)

"But Honey, you've got to eat it," I said to my eight-year-old daughter Stephanie. "We caught it, cleaned it, and cooked it just for you. We can't waste it."

"It's icky and it smells like fish," she said. She tightened her lips in stubborn defiance.

"It's icky and it smells like fish because it is fish," I said. "On camping trips real outdoorsmen have to eat all kinds of icky food. But this is good. See, it hardly has any dirt or bugs in it."

She looked a little closer.

"What's that thing with the crooked legs and bent wings?" she asked.

"Where? Oh that little thing? I'll just spoon it out. See?"

"It probably died because it ate some of the fish," she said.

"It's okay, you don't have to eat it," my wife Dawn intervened. "We'll roast some marshmallows later."

"How about you boys?" I asked, looking elsewhere for support. "You liked the fish didn't you? There's plenty if you want more."

"I'm stuffed," said Matt.

"Couldn't eat another bite," said Sean.

"I'll have some," said Brian, his mouth still full.

Good old Brian. I knew he wouldn't let me down. When he was a toddler, we used to have to check his mouth regularly for small pebbles, pieces of sticks, and slow crawling insects in the larval stage. And we had to be careful he didn't bite our fingers when we were doing it. Brian would eat anything.

I was the designated chef on all the family campouts. That was a concession I'd made to Dawn early in our marriage.

"If you're going to drag me to all of these uncomfortable places with no bathrooms just to swat bugs and to sleep on the cold, damp ground, then don't expect me to do any cooking or to wash any dishes," she had said.

That was fine with me. Lunches were easy. We usually just threw some sandwiches together and ate on the run. For breakfasts my specialty was boiling water to pour over instant oatmeal. I'd tried other options with varying degrees of success.

"I didn't want scrambled eggs," Stephanie complained. "I said I wanted pancakes."

"Those are pancakes," I said. "They just look like scrambled eggs. My pancakes are special. You can eat them with a spoon. Pour lots of syrup on them and they'll taste just like Mom made them."

"There are bugs in the syrup too."

"We can't waste it," I said. "You've got to eat it."

"It's okay Honey," Dawn intervened again. "I'll get some sugar-coated Corn Crunchies cereal for you."

"I'll eat her pancakes," Brian offered.

Dinners were more complicated because I was expected to actually cook something. Sometimes I could get away with dumping something into a pot and firing up the camp stove. If I had to throw some burgers or hot dogs over some charcoal it was still no problem.

Grilling chicken took longer if I was expected to marinate it or to splash barbecue sauce on it while it cooked. The tricky part about my chicken was eating it. First you had to scrape off the charred part. Then you had to bite carefully so you wouldn't sink your teeth all the way down to the raw part.

If I got really ambitious, I'd come up with a special dish, as long as it didn't take more than one pot or pan to prepare it. The goal was to have as few things to wash as possible.

"This spaghetti looks like it has chunks of oatmeal in it," Sean said.

"Yuck, mine too," Matt said.

"I ate mine already," Brian said.

"Did you boil the pasta in this morning's dish water again?" Dawn asked.

"Impossible," I said.

"We were in a hurry this morning," Matt said.

"It's possible then," Sean said.

"And you hate to do dishes Dad," Matt said.

"That makes it very likely then," Sean said.

"What's the big deal?" Brian said.

"Maybe if someone would help me with the camp chores this wouldn't happen," I said.

"Mom!" Stephanie shouted.

"I'll get the cereal Honey," Dawn said.

"Get some for me too," I said.

When you hunt or fish, you're expected to eat your catch from time to time.

The best way to prepare wild game or fish is to place all of your ingredients – veggies, seasonings, everything -- in an aluminum foil packet and toss it on a bed of coals. Leave it there until you can't stand it any longer, and then fetch it out of the fire with a long stick.

You won't have any dishes to wash and if you're lucky, you'll be able to salvage some edible, if not recognizable, portion.

Besides, recognizable is not always desirable. I used to boil all small game in a large pot first, because then it was easier to get the meat off of the bone. Then one time Stephanie shrieked when she saw little squirrel skeletons rising to the surface of the murky water. Sean didn't help matters when he told her they were her pet guinea pigs.

Once the meat was in unrecognizable, non-animal shaped chunks and placed in a stew or a can of beans, Stephanie was fine. She'd still poke around with her spoon, looking for crooked legs, bent wings and other bug parts, but the meat didn't bother her.

When you're with other hunters or fishermen, you don't always have control over what's on the menu, or how it's prepared. That's why it's a good idea to have a wild game and fish survival kit that includes containers of salt, ground pepper, chili powder, garlic powder, onion powder, ground cayenne pepper, some spicy horseradish mustard and a large bottle of ketchup.

If you can't disguise the taste with spices or if you keep getting images of squirrel skeletons in murky water, remember, you don't really have to eat it. A couple of handfuls of sugar-coated Corn Crunchies ought to hold you until oatmeal in the morning.

My Family
In Fishing History

(Originally published by Game & Fish Publications, April 2002)

History is full of mistakes. It stands to reason. In order to find the best way to do anything, you have to eliminate all of the wrong ways.

Advances in fishing have depended on this trial-and-error method. I come from a long line of fishing innovators. If you look back at any point in the history of fishing, you will find one of my ancestors hard at work making errors and diligently adding to the long list of the wrong ways to do things.

One of the earliest was Glurb Barlow, who lived back when my family tree was a mere sprout struggling to poke its way out of the earth. His hunting and fishing exploits were chronicled in the most elaborate cave paintings of his day. It was Glurb, incidentally, who first coined the phrase, "You can bring a mastodon to water, but you can't make him drink."

Since he lived before fishing line was invented, Glurb did all of his fishing with his trusty spear. It was Glurb who first experimented extensively with live bait.

He collected handfuls of leeches, grubs, worms and caterpillars, then experimented by tossing them one or two at a time into his favorite fishing hole while standing patiently with spear in hand.

Then, suddenly, in a moment of genius, Glurb had a thought. He shouldn't be using leeches, grubs, worms and caterpillars at all. It didn't make sense to throw away the

41

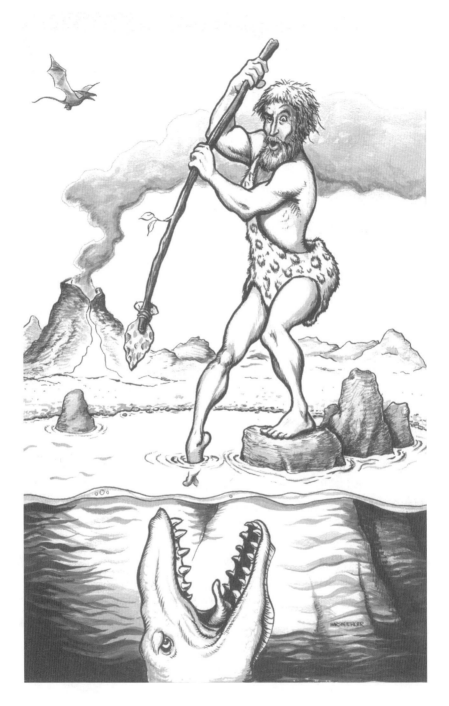

tastiest side dishes in the hopes of catching the main course.

So Glurb simply stuck his foot in the water and began to wiggle his toes. This was a courageous thing to do back then, not only because the Ice Age was approaching and the water was quite cold, but because most of the species of fish back then had rather large teeth.

This innovative approach to fishing brought him nothing but ridicule. "There goes Two-Toes Glurb," they would shout.

It is said that one day Glurb saw something moving beneath the surface and hurled his spear with deadly accuracy.

It's possible that this incident marked the beginning of what was to become a cruel family curse, as each Barlow has literally or figuratively shot himself in the foot one way or another ever since.

After Glurb came Bonsai Barlow who tried floating on a log to get to the fish he couldn't reach from shore. He was swept away in the rapids, but returned two years later for a second attempt.

This time he anchored the log with a heavy rock and a vine that was tied securely around his ankle. He drowned of course, but at least he had solved the problem of being swept down the rapids, so there was some feeling that progress had been made.

Years later, fishing line was invented and it was a Barlow who first mastered the art of tangling it into a useless wad of knots, loops and twists. So it was only appropriate that another Barlow came along to invent the reel to hold those gobs of line.

The Barlow Reel never really caught on, however. It wasn't until much later, when some other person by chance positioned the reel near the handle of the rod instead of the tip that fishermen used them in any great numbers.

And so it went over the centuries until at last it was my turn to place yet another indelible blotch on the sport of fishing, all in the name of family tradition. It wasn't easy. In order to become a true innovator of the fishing faux pas, you first have to study the classics.

After years of tedious repetition, I can now perform respectable renditions of some old-time favorites. I can flip a quadruple loop of fly line around a tree branch on my backcast with my eyes closed.

Actually, since my fly casting resembles an 1800's teamster cracking a rawhide whip on a team of mules, everyone in the vicinity would do well to close their eyes and cover their faces.

With a spinning rod, I can inadvertently hook a fisherman on the other side of a stream nine casts out of ten. "Oops, hey, it's me again. Sorry. Just cut the line and keep the lure this time." I'm so good at that one, I've been threatened with bodily harm numerous times.

I finally decided my best contribution to fishing's bad ideas would be equipment oriented, rather than some innovative technique.

My best effort to date has been my reversible chest waders. The idea is to be able to easily peel the waders off, even if it means turning them inside out like an old sweat sock in the process, which wouldn't matter since both sides would be the same.

I demonstrated how easy it is to take these waders off to a delighted crowd at the county fair one year, but several people were quick to point out that I really should have remembered to wear something underneath.

They say that insanity in a family often skips a generation. If that's true, then I can rest easy because my kids, God bless them, are absolutely nuts. My kids all have what you might call "Square One" personalities.

They are skeptical of history, have a mistrust of instructions verbal or written, and are oblivious to the fact that there are long-established ways to do things properly thanks to generations of Barlows who have already established the wrong ways.

Simply put, they have to start everything at "Square One," trying things on their own and working out the procedures themselves.

One summer, I gave new rod and reel combos to my boys, Curly, Larry, and Moe. After some brief instruction, we went down to Little Stump Lake to try to catch some sunnies and bluegills.

Within 20 minutes, the new rods were discarded and the boys were having the time of their lives leaning over the dock and trying to scoop up the fish with a net, a plastic jar, and their bare hands. Glurb would have been proud.

Tackle Box
Psychology

(Originally published by Game & Fish Publications, June 1997)

Fishing is popular because it soothes such a wide variety of mental disorders in so many of us.

I came to that conclusion last year while fishing Little Stump Lake with Henry "Gills" Gillespie, a fishing fanatic who was unstable enough mentally to really take advantage of everything fishing had to offer.

It was the first weekend of the bass season and the lake was full of boats.

"Look at all of these people," I said, thinking aloud. "All shapes, sizes, races, religions, socio-economic classes. Fishing appeals to them all. They're all here."

"Yeah, and I wish they were somewhere else," Gills said. "Then maybe the fishing would be better."

I must have snapped him out of his own philosophical reverie. He stopped picking his nose and reached into the cooler.

"There has to be more to it than just trying to catch fish," I said. "I think fishing is mankind's universal time-out. It's the salve for whatever ails us. It gives us the opportunity to momentarily ease the stresses of our everyday concerns. Food for thought, huh?"

"Exactly what I was thinking," Gills said. "You want a piece of this sandwich?"

"No thanks. You see, if catching fish was the main point,

we'd become commercial fishermen and use nets. Or we'd buy our fish directly from hatcheries, instead of wasting everybody's time by stocking them by the thousands, then trying to catch them back one at a time, only to release them after the effort. No, you can't just take it for what it appears on the surface."

"I don't know," Gills said. "That scrawny little guy over there just took one off the surface using some kind of a plug, looks like."

"There must be a type of fishing to suit everyone's sense of well-being," I said. "You start kids out fishing for panfish because they're plentiful and easy to catch. It's fun, sure, but more important, it's a confidence builder.

"Some guys tie their own flies to present to wary, finicky trout. That satisfies the need in some for artistic fulfillment. At the same time it provides some intellectual challenge. And having a bass strike your surface lure can bring a thrill, a bit of adventure to your otherwise dreary existence.

"The key is to find the type of fishing that is compatible and beneficial to your specific emotional and mental deficiencies. Crappies, trout, walleyes, catfish, muskies, pike, bass -- they all satisfy the different psychological needs of the people who fish for them."

"I need to catch another bass soon," Gills said, "because if I just sit here guzzling down these diet sodas," he paused to belch, "I'm going to need to go to the bathroom."

"You know," I said, "I'd even go so far as to say that an expert could decipher the psychological make-up of a person merely by looking in his tackle box."

"This tackle box is a mess," Gills said. "I think if I switch from a black wiggler to a chartreuse crawler, I might change my luck."

"I'm no Sherlock Holmes," I said, "but let's see what you've got there. Now don't get mad. Remember this is just an intellectual exercise.

"First, look at the way everything's just thrown in the tackle box. There's no sense of organization in the placement of lures by design, size, color or anything. There are gobs of tangled line here and there and, look, a leaky packet of ketchup from some fast-food restaurant.

"From that we can probably determine that this person is an unmotivated, sloppy, person of limited intelligence, who is mostly likely overweight as well."

Gills tried to pull down his stained tee-shirt so that it would cover the belt-overhang portion of his belly.

"Let's see what else we have here," I continued. "Ah ha! An old skateboard wheel, a wad of bubble gum under one outside corner, an unfilled entry form for the Little Stump Lake Bass Tournament -- five years old -- with a grocery list scrawled on the back.

"This speaks volumes. Here's a person saddled with children and driven hard by an unsympathetic, demanding wife. He has probably achieved nothing during a lackluster career and is trying to make up for his lack of competitiveness in the business world by trying to compete against other fishermen.

"He's duping himself into believing that he can salvage some semblance of his self-respect and manhood by catching a bigger fish than the guy next to him. Pitiful. Yet, as we see, the form has not been filled out, showing this person to have a profound fear of failure."

"I'm afraid the chartreuse crawler isn't working, either," Gills said. "I'm going to switch to a jig and pork rind and move the boat closer to the shoreline drop-off."

"I may be going out on a limb here," I said, "but I would venture to say that this person is an emotional basket-case, full of whining excuses for not getting things done, a person who probably over-reacts to the slightest, insignificant accomplishment with ego-building, pompous celebration."

"Yee haw! Look at this granddaddy of all bass," Gills

shouted. "That makes it, what, three for me and how many for you? None? Oh well, it's lucky for you I came along. Otherwise you wouldn't know what a bass looks like, Stevie-boy. Yee haw!"

"Okay, wise-guy," I said. "You've had your laugh. I've caught plenty of bass on this lake and you know it. Conditions just weren't right and you were lucky, that's all.

"I'd show you a thing or two about fishing," I said, "but right now we've got to start heading back. The kids have to go to soccer practice and Dawn will have my hide if I'm late."

Gills was unusually quiet on the way back for a guy who normally had a lot to say when he caught more fish. He wasn't an overly sensitive person, but I thought maybe I'd gone overboard with my tackle box analysis.

"By the way, Gills, no offense on all that other stuff I said earlier, right?"

"No offense," Gills said. "That was your tackle box."

49

My Brushes
With Death

(Originally published by Game & Fish Publications, March 1993)

"He stopped momentarily to check his rifle. Only three cartridges left. They would have to do. These mountains were so cold and unforgiving. He leaned into the howling wind and trudged on through the snow. He was near exhaustion, but he had to find his hunting partners. It was up to him and him alone..."

I was so absorbed in pecking away at the computer keyboard with two thumbs and a forefinger that I didn't hear my wife, Dawn, sneak into the den.

"What are you doing?" she asked. I shot from my chair like a flushed partridge.

"Writing my memoirs," I explained as I climbed down from atop my gun cabinet. "How's this for a title: My Brushes with Death and Other Adventures of the Great Outdoors, the Dramatized True Life Exploits of a Seasoned, Veteran Woodsman..."

"All that's the title?"

"Don't interrupt, I'm not finished. Where was I? Oh, yeah, Seasoned, Veteran Woodsman, the Shocking Revelations of Life in the Wilds of North America, One Man's Saga of Courage and Resourcefulness in the Face of Adversity, subtitled: I Hunted Alone, I Fished by Myself."

"So familiar with Mother Nature, you simply called her Mom?"

"Don't laugh. This could be an important literary work. At the very least my reminiscences will be a lasting legacy for our children.

"So they can learn from your mistakes?"

"Funny. I think they'll enjoy reading about my daring adventures, which in some small way aren't that different from the life and death challenges faced by all the great explorers and pioneers through the ages."

"Oh, so it's a work of fiction."

"Hardly. I'm drawing most of my stuff from the journals I've kept over the years."

"Wait here," she said. "I'll be right back."

I started my journals several years ago with the intent to gather data on patterns of animal behavior in the areas I hunted and fished.

I kept track of dates, times and weather conditions. I jotted down signs and sightings of game. When fishing, I noted water temperature, depth, and the lures that were successful.

"Besides documenting my adventures," I told Dawn when she returned, "I can use the data in these journals to my advantage. For example, my entry of May 17, 1989, reads:

'Weather clear, air temperature 65 degrees, water temperature 50 degrees at 20 feet. Trolled an imitation minnow at that depth through the narrows on Little Stump Lake at about 7:30 am. Caught an 18-inch rainbow trout, marking the 20th time this lure has been successful here in these conditions.'"

Dawn, meanwhile, had brought out a little book with a floral print cloth cover and was thumbing through it.

"What's that?" I asked.

"My diary," she said. She selected an entry, cleared her throat and read: "May 17, 1989. Spent the morning reviewing the stock market reports, while Steve went fishing on the lake. He came home completely discouraged and threw that old imitation minnow in the trash. He said he caught Fred again in the narrows, but released him. That makes about a dozen times he's caught the same fish -- the only fish he's ever caught with that lure. He said that since he's known Fred since he was a fingerling, he didn't have the heart to keep him now that he was legal size."

"Okay, so instead of learning certain times to catch lots of fish, I ended up learning how to catch certain fish lots of times," I said. "But what about hunting?" I flipped through my journals. "Here, listen to this: 'November 28, 1987. Rained all day. No deer spotted. Convinced deer not active in these conditions.'"

"November 28, 1987," Dawn countered with her diary entry. "Rained all day. I scanned the want ads in the hopes of finding a real job for Steve. From the window I saw several deer passing through the field by the edge of the hardwoods behind our house. I called to Steve in the den, but he said it was third down and long and inside of two minutes to go and I should wait until halftime with whatever was so important.'

"Between your journals and my diary," she said, "I think we're revealing less about animal behavior and more about your behavior."

She patted me on the head reassuringly, the way she always did with our dog, Brutus, after she felt guilty for yelling at him for digging holes in the back yard. "I know you can't help it," she'd tell him. "That's just the way you are."

"Okay, I admit that these journals haven't yielded any breakthroughs in hunting or fishing techniques. But they still serve as a record of my adventures afield. I believe that everyone who hunts or fishes has a bit of the adventurer inside. There's always that urge to explore what's over the next rise, to witness nature's hidden woodland sights, to probe the depths in hopes of latching onto a monster of a fish, to..."

"To boldly go where no man has gone before, right?"

"Be honest, now," I said. "You have to admit that I've had some pretty exciting exploits over the years. How about our canoe adventure on the rapids at Satan's Stairwell? How about my showdown with death in Bear Swamp? How about..."

"Those were more misadventures than adventures."

"Well, how about the one I'm writing now? The Icy Ordeal on Signal Mountain?" I turned toward the typewriter. "'He leaned into the howling wind and trudged on through the snow. He was near exhaustion, but he had to find his hunting partners. It was up to him and him alone...'"

"Honey, you were the one lost that time on Signal Mountain."

"I'll mention that in a few pages. I'm allowed some creative license. This is a dramatization, remember. Imagination plays a part in all great outdoor adventures."

She patted me on the head reassuringly. "I know you can't help it," she said. "That's just the way you are."

Give Me
A Little Credit

(Originally published by Game & Fish Publications, March 1992)

Sales had been slow at the North American Outdoor Recreation Exposition and Flea Market until I showed up with my brother-in-law, Floyd.

The moment we walked in, the eyes of every salesman were on us. It was if they could sense that my money was burning a hole in Floyd's pocket.

Neither one of us alone could have wrestled so much as a business card from one of these guys. Floyd had the eager look of a hound on a hare. But any experienced salesman knew immediately that Floyd didn't have a dime.

I didn't have a dime, either, but I had something more important: credit. My good credit rating, together with Floyd's eagerness to exploit it, made us easy prey.

I fully intended to get out of there without buying anything except a one-dollar mystery grab bag at Vern's Fishing Tackle Emporium booth.

Those grab bags were guaranteed to contain at least five dollars worth of overstocked fishing lures. In 1972 I bought one and used the Super-Flash Electro-Wiggleys inside to finish third in the Little Stump Lake Hunting and Fishing Club's annual bass tournament the year of the hurricane.

Since then I have bought a mystery grab bag every year and although I've never matched the trememdous results of 1972, I still feel I owe something to Vern's Fishing Tackle

Emporium for securing my place in fishing history.

On the way to Vern's display, Floyd wanted to stop and look at a display of hunting rifles.

"Hey, listen to this," he said. "We can get a new rifle with a synthetic stock custom-fitted while we wait."

"How much?" I asked.

"Never ask how much," Floyd said. "You never need to know the price unless you're going to pay for it all up front. This is the age of the installment plan."

I had wanted a new hunting rifle. And my old rifle with the beat-up stock was in such deplorable shape that Floyd was sure he could screw a light bulb into the muzzle and sell it as one of those expensive driftwood lamps.

The salesman tossed boxes aside until he found the proper rifle, dusted it off and handed it to me.

"I think it's a bit long," I said.

"Nonsense. It was made for you."

"I can't reach the trigger."

"Important safety feature."

"How much is it?"

"$33.95 a month, nothing down, nothing due for six months."

Well that price didn't seem too bad. I could cut back on a few expenses and make ends meet. Next Floyd wanted to stop to look at new fishing boats.

"My friends and I are always knocking elbows when we borrow your boat," Floyd said. "You really could use a bigger one."

So the cost of the new boat came to $232.50 per month. It was loaded with everything the salesman said an experienced angler such as myself needed. Of course the deluxe, no-sway trailer was $67.48 per month extra, but as Floyd said, you can't expect them to give the things away.

Still between Vern's Fishing Tackle Emporium and us were displays of R.V.s, four-wheel-drive trucks, camping equipment and mountain bikes.

It made sense to get the R.V. that sleeps six because it was only $42.07 per month more than the one that sleeps four. Now we could take those extended hunting and fishing trips in comfort, provided of course that I could get the time off from working to pay for it all. Floyd promised he'd take lots of photos and send me a postcard once in a while so I wouldn't miss a thing.

The four-wheel-drive truck was a good idea. I needed something to tow the boat and on short excursions I might not want to take the R.V. even if Floyd wasn't using it.

I got special prices on the camping gear and mountain bikes. You've got to buy when you see a great deal, Floyd had pointed out. If you hesitate, you end up spending more money in the long run.

At Vern's Fishing Tackle Emporium display we had to wait for Vern to take care of another customer. I decided to add up my monthly payments so I could show my wife, Dawn, that she wasn't the only one who could save loads of money.

I suppose $2,000 plus change every month is not a large sum of money if you have no other expenses and you don't mind eating infrequently.

"I'm not worried," Floyd said. "You're the one who signed his name to everything. They can't touch me. Listen, now that you have a new truck and a new boat, you can sell your old car and old boat to make the first couple of payments on the R.V.

"The first payment on the new boat isn't due for six months. You can rent it and the R.V. to your friends to make the first payment. At the end of the hunting season you can sell the new rifle -- it doesn't fit you anyway -- to make a quick payment before they repossess the truck.

"You can keep switching credit card companies to buy some time, but they'll catch you eventually. Or you can get one of those bill consolidation loans. That way you'll have only one company trying to track you down to have you arrested. If you keep traveling in the R.V., they may never find you.

"If things don't work out you can sell everything off. Even then you would have had the use of all of this fantastic equipment for nearly a year at the cost of only the few thousand you'd lose in depreciation.

"Or you can keep some of this stuff and sell your house. That shouldn't be a problem because Dawn is going to leave you anyway when she finds out what you did. Then you can live in your R.V. and ride your mountain bike to work. You always wanted to live the life of a nomad. You could camp year-around. Look at the bright side."

I was frozen like a buck in a headlight beam. I knew trouble was coming, but I couldn't get out of its way.

"Hey, snap out of it," Vern said. "You want your mystery grab bag? I had to raise the price to two dollars this year."

"What?" I said, as I came back to my senses. "You've got to be kidding, Vern. Two dollars for only five dollars worth of lures? Forget it." I started to walk away, but stopped. "Hey Vern, you still looking to rent an R.V. this summer?"

Picture This

(Originally published by Game & Fish Publications, September 1991)

I've been devoting a lot of time lately to sharpening my skills as an outdoor photographer. Look carefully at the photos on this page. These represent all of my magazine-quality photos to date.

Okay, stop looking. I know what you're saying and you're right. There are no photos on this page. You have to realize that it's very difficult getting those close-up, candid shots of animals going about their daily business of making a living.

I used to think that I could, with a little patience, take the same kind of wildlife shots you see in outdoor magazines. I imagined that even the roughest days of a professional photographer would still be quite glamorous.

"Okay, everybody, let's line up for those deer-grazing-in-the-meadow shots we rehearsed yesterday. Hey, you there, don't you know the cutesy Bambi look is out? I'm sorry, we can't use you. I ask for trophy deer and look what they send me.

"You, yes you with the big rack. Let's get some shots of you rubbing the bark off that sapling there. Yeah, that's it. More emotion now. The rut's almost here. Fierce now. Show me fierce. Great. Aw, nuts. The sun went behind a cloud. That's it today, folks. We lost the light. Let's do lunch. I don't know how they expect me to work in these horrible conditions."

There are many benefits of outdoor photography. By creating a photo history of your outdoor experiences, you not only preserve your memories for years to come, but you can pinpoint your weaknesses. This was apparent the other night when I selected a couple of dozen photo albums to show my brother, Gary.

"Look at my shot of the ten-point buck on this page," I said. I prodded him with an elbow to the ribs until he stopped snoring and opened his eyes.

I could tell my outdoor photos were getting him excited about the upcoming hunting season. My brother often feigns sleeping on his deer stand, too, to lull unsuspecting deer into a feeling of false security.

"I don't see any ten-point buck," he said, squinting at the page.

"Oh, wait." I wiped a fleck of dust off the photo. "There he is."

"That brown speck?"

"A real beauty, but a bit far away, perhaps."

Outdoor photography is a lot like hunting and fishing. You can always blame your lack of success on your equipment and use it as an excuse to buy more.

"I'm trying to talk Dawn into converting some of her blue chip stocks into a new zoom lens." I glanced at my wife, who was bending over to lift more photo albums onto the coffee table. "Maybe even a wide-angle."

The nice thing about Dawn is that she would never strike me in front of my brother. Instead she just smiled that wait-until-later smile.

"I do have some close-up shots, though. Look at these." I turned the page.

"This one's just a blur," Gary said.

"Shudder release," I said.

"Don't you mean shutter release?"

"No. Shudder release. It's a strange phenomenon, not unlike buck fever, known to all novice wildlife photographers. You just get a chance at the photo of a lifetime and you start

59

shaking uncontrollably."

"If your camera jumps around that much, think of what the barrel of your rifle is doing each season."

"That's not the worst of it," I said. "Look closely at the far edge of this photo. See that? That's the tip of a tail."

"No wonder you always miss."

"It's not me. I took that new camera back to the shop and told the guy it wasn't sighted-in properly. But he didn't want to hear anything about it. You know how they are once they make a sale." I placed another album in front of him.

"Feet?" he said. "You have two pages of pictures of feet?"

"Great, huh? I call this layout, 'The Shoes of the Fisherman.' It all started when I accidentally tripped the shutter when I was trying to get to the front of my boat. Then I realized what I had stumbled on."

"The anchor?"

"No, silly. Don't you see? I've found my niche. Some photographers take close-ups of frost on leaves or dew drops on spider webs to convey subtle messages about life and the cost of film processing. I think these photos, especially the ones of my old work boots, make a strong, obvious statement about the whole fishing experience."

My brother shook his head, in awe, I think.

"I saved the best for last." I handed him the final album. He flipped page after page.

"These are all pictures of you in your boat, holding up your fishing rod and a bare hook," he said. "Who took these photos, anyway?"

"I did. I bolted a tripod to the back to the boat and used that handy self-timer feature on the camera. For some reason nobody has wanted to go fishing with me since I started bringing my camera along. Jealousy over my artistic talents, I guess. But look at the captions."

"Lunker largemouth bass, trophy brown trout, world record muskellunge," he read aloud. "But there aren't any fish

60

in these photos, just bare hooks. Don't tell me, catch and release, right?"

"Almost," I said. "These are photos of 'the ones that got away.' No one would believe me if I told fish stories without proof. Now I have photographic evidence."

"I think you've fallen overboard one too many times," he said. "And this has to be costing you a fortune."

"Actually I'm breaking about even because of the photos I'm selling."

"Someone's going to publish your photos?"

"No, but I sold one to my friend, Pete. It was a really good shot of him cozying up to that redheaded waitress at the Gone Fish Inn on the last trip we took. Funny guy, that Pete, but his wife has no sense of humor. So I kept the negative and it's sure to bring in a little something every month."

The Truth About
Fishing With Kids

(Originally published by Game & Fish Publications, July 1991)

5 a.m. I peeked out from behind the closet door -- all clear. It looked as if my pre-dawn raid to grab my fishing gear would be successful. But the minute I stepped out I was confronted by my three-year-old son, Sean.

"We going fishin' Dad?" he asked.

I looked down on that smiling, innocent, gullible face. How could I deceive him?

"Well, son, not exactly," I said. "You see Mr. Cooper next door wants to borrow this stuff and ...," and I could see myself feeling guilty about my little fib all day long as I reeled in lunker after lunker from the lake.

Sean rushed out of the room screaming for reinforcements, "Hey guys, we going fishin'!"

At the kitchen table Sean's brothers, Matt, 8, and Brian, 6, were already dressed and eating breakfast. Their rods and tackle boxes were ready and waiting by the back door.

I suspected some counter-intelligence agent had tipped the kids off about my covert operation. Just then she scuffed into the kitchen wearing a flannel nightgown, terrycloth bathrobe and oversized, bunny rabbit slippers. It was my wife, Dawn, in her summer sleeping apparel.

"I'll be ready in a jiffy." She yawned. We hit the road just after lunch.

Much has been written about fishing with children, the joys

of sharing moments outdoors with your kids, of introducing them to nature. But stop the violins. Snap out of that reverie for a moment. Let's get down to the nuts and bolts, the realities of fishing with children.

First of all memorize this axiom: If you want a nice family outing, take the kids fishing. But if you want to go fishing, leave the family out.

Don't get me wrong. I wouldn't trade my family for anything, not even a new, fully-equipped bass boat, though I might be tempted if I had my choice of colors. It's just that the two are not compatible.

When you take the kids fishing you never get to fish yourself since you spend so much time untangling line, baiting hooks, and dislodging lures from submerged logs and exposed flesh -- in short, most of the things you'd be doing on your own and calling it fun, but sheer agony when multiplied by the number of people in your family.

Add to that skipping stones, netting minnows, diving after bullfrogs, and individual trips to the bathroom since they never all have to go at the same time.

To top it off they aren't old enough to fully comprehend the wisdom of your years when you tell them, "The reason you kids are catching all the fish and Daddy hasn't caught one is due to the lake's unique stratification of the thermal layers that adversely affects the appetites of these particular species when presented lures cast with increased accuracy, distance and velocity by an experienced angler. In layman's terms, you guys have beginner's luck."

In a few years, when the kids will be in their teens, it won't be much better. They'll be more independent, sure, but that only makes fishing with them impossible. At that age they will be more interested in posters of rock stars and simply won't want the things you have, such as downriggers, depth finders, a mortgage, car payments and high credit card bills.

At the same time you'll be at the age where you might

want, but can't have the things they have, such as teenage girlfriends.

Later on in life, if the kids are still within a day's drive, they may not have the time or the inclination to fish with you even if you still do have some of your own teeth. Besides, they would still catch all the fish while you would be the one now making frequent trips to the bathroom.

And if you dared to mention your theory on the statification of thermal layers, they might take it as further evidence of your impending senility.

Sound depressing? That's why, realizing the futility of taking the kids fishing at any age, I was trying to sneak out of the house at 5 a.m. to go fishing by myself.

If you do opt for the family outing or if you have a wife with oversized bunny rabbit slippers and therefore have no choice, all is not lost. Simply resign yourself to the fact that you won't be doing any fishing that day, relax and enjoy watching the children as they grow.

To make the most of the occasion you might want to follow these fishing-with-kids guidelines:

1. Always use live bait. Catching it can be an outing in itself. Any disgusting low life form that crawls or slithers along the ground is excellent since the kids will become interested in playing with the bait if the fish aren't biting.

2. If you don't have the time to procure live bait, grab the leftovers from last night's dinner. Let's face it, fish are relatively stupid animals and, like yourself, are apt to have short memories of your wife's cooking prowess and will take the bait time after time.

In an emergency you'll have provisions to tide you over, a benefit you don't get with the disgusting low life forms mentioned above. That brings us to:

3. Bring plenty to eat and drink, especially if you fish by boat. Every time one of the kids in the front of the boat wants to try a different lure, throw a sandwich. That will keep the

child quiet temporarily and before long all of your kids will weigh so much you won't dare take them fishing for fear of exceeding the gross weight capacity of the vessel.

4. Bring gadgets to keep their interest. Forget the romantic simplicity of a cane pole and string. Kids love gadgets as much as you do. After all, kids are just outdoor lovers who haven't reached their full potential, just as we, as outdoors lovers, have never reached our full potential because we still act like kids.

Give them reels to jam, lures to lose and tackle boxes to drop overboard. The key here is to make sure you leave your own tackle at home. Make them break their own equipment. This way they'll gain a full appreciation of the joys of fishing firsthand and with any luck will not ask to go along the next time you try to sneak out of the house at 5 a.m.

Advice For All
You Losers

(Originally published by Game & Fish Publications, December 1994)

I'm a loser. My wife, Dawn, told me so and she's right. You see, I believe there are two types of people in this world: those who are finders and keepers and those who are losers and weepers.

I fall into the latter category because I'm always losing stuff. The outdoors is virtually littered with things that I've lost -- a fillet knife here, a compass there, a beautiful new hunting cap somewhere, I don't know where.

The finders and keepers of this world owe their good fortune largely to people like me who lose things. Finders are those who, if blindfolded, spun around and then turned loose in a field, would stop to find at their feet an odd assortment of money, four-leaf clovers, and the pair of binoculars with the broken strap that I lost a week ago.

Finders and keepers are the ones who as kids in the park were always able to find the foul ball hit into the tall grass where I could find only -- to be polite -- where the dog was walked that morning.

Finders seem to be lucky all their lives. Losers are incurable. As a schoolboy I used to lose my homework and my lunch money. Now I still lose my lunch money, along with fly fishing reels, flashlights, and camera lens caps.

There are many ways to lose things and I'm expert in them

all. The most mysterious, but sure way to lose something is to put it in a safe place where you know you can find it later.

Of course when you go to look for it later, you won't be able to remember where that safe place was. All is not lost, however. In 90 percent of these mysterious disappearances, the item, whether it's you watch, pocket knife or favorite bass lure, will be recovered freshly laundered and neatly put away in your sock drawer.

The most common way, of course, is to momentarily set something down. If you are a loser, never set anything down.

On a typical hunt, there are several times when I will stop, take off my daypack and search for something I want, but can't find, such as a candy bar, canteen, or map of the way home.

Invariably I'll take off my gloves and put them on a rock or a log -- some heavy object that I'm sure not to lose. If I should find what I'm looking for in my pack, chances are I'll walk off overjoyed at the rare victory, never giving a thought to my gloves on the rock or log.

Then, after noticing a certain numbness in my fingers, I'll backtrack to the rock or log, only to find my gloves are gone. Why are they gone? The explanation could lie in the fact that so many rocks and logs look alike and that maybe I'm looking in the wrong places.

Lately, I'm beginning to suspect something more sinister, such as a thieving flock of crows or a marauding band of squirrels making a nice living dealing in used sporting goods and just waiting for me to make a mistake and set something down. I've often wondered how many birds were hatched or how many nuts were stored in that blaze orange hunting cap I lost.

Another way to effortlessly lose things is to wear pants with shallow pockets. If you opt for deeper pockets, you tend to cram more into them and then lose things that spill out as you dig for what you want in the bottom.

You can get pockets with buttons, but you'll inevitably lose the buttons. You can use zippers to seal pockets like a vault at the top, only to lose things out of the hole in the bottom. The only saving grace about pockets is that you can always blame the loss of items on the failure of the pocket rather than your own absent-minded tendencies.

You can prevent losing things from your pants pockets by stowing everything in a fanny pack. Just don't lose the fanny pack, which I suppose could be easier than losing your pants pockets, which you could only accomplish by losing your pants. I know those who've done it, but we can't discuss that here.

Others have made an attempt at loss prevention by attaching everything they carry afield to strings, ropes, bands, lanyards and chains.

Just loop your camera, binoculars, compass, and whistle around your neck, dangle your flashlight and canteen from your pack, suspend your knives and other essentials from your belt and sling your rifle or shotgun over your shoulder. Fasten your gloves to your sleeves as your mother did for you when you were a neophyte loser.

When fishing, tie down your tackle boxes, cooler, and anything else you don't want overboard because water attracts sporting goods like a magnet. The deeper the water, the greater the likelihood of dropping something into it.

If, at the end of it all, you don't hang yourself, you're sure to feel like a tangled marionette.

Often it's best to just resign yourself to the fact that you are a loser and learn to carry three or four of each of the small items that you are apt to lose during an excursion outdoors.

This strategy can really weigh you down. Remember, no matter how much spills out of the pockets of your pack during a hike, your pack will never feel any lighter.

Label everything with your name and address. This will encourage finders and keepers to return lost items to you.

However, thieving crows and marauding squirrels will see no moral dilemma in finding and keeping your labeled possessions since they can't read.

You would think there would be advantages to losing things. Lucky is the loser who manages to lose -– as if on purpose -- only old, worn equipment that he wants replaced on Christmas. As Christmas approaches, you can take inventory of your hunting and fishing gear, list items to be replaced, then lose the list where loved ones are sure to find it.

Be sure to specify that you want nothing in camouflage, which was invented by a ruthless finder and keeper to take advantage of losers and weepers.

What happens if, while losing the usual array of equipment during a hunt, you become lost yourself?

First of all, let's set the record straight. You can never lose yourself. You know where you are. You're standing knee deep in the exact center of some mosquito-infested swamp, miles from the nearest road, directly beneath a threatening rain cloud, just one half hour from total darkness. It's your camp, your truck, and the rest of the civilized world you've misplaced.

The enlightened loser might think he can simply follow his own trail of dropped and lost equipment to find his way back. This is called the Hansel and Gretel Theory. It seldom works when you're alone because as a loser, you rarely find something you've lost.

You can enlist a finder and keeper as a hunting partner. When you become lost you can, in a nonchalant manner not letting on that you've misplaced civilization, ask your finder and keeper friend to help you to locate your gloves, hat, ammunition and fanny pack in succession until you've hiked back to your starting point.

The trouble is that when you've misplaced civilization you very often have misplaced your hunting partner as well. Then, while you are out there trying to pick up your trail of dropped and lost items, your finder and keeper hunting partner is over the next ridge finding and picking up those things you've lost and obliterating your path home.

If you're lucky enough to find your way back to your truck, then you must begin the search through shallow, buttonless pockets and deep, zippered pockets with holes in them to find your keys.

And do you know where you might eventually find them? Check back home in your sock drawer.

No Man
On An Island

(Originally published by Game & Fish Publications, July 1992)

One weekend my wife, Dawn, was cleaning house by systematically throwing away all of my prized possessions when she came across something that seemed to puzzle her.

"What's this piece of driftwood with the notch in one end?" she asked.

"That's our Swiss Family Robinson calendar, remember? We started it when we were stranded on the island last summer."

"Some calendar. There's only one notch on it."

"Okay, so we only spent one night on the island. But we could have spent our last days there, huddled for warmth over the fading embers of our signal fire, while we waited to starve to death."

It had all started as a family fishing trip on a lake about a two-hours' drive to the north. We planned on canoeing to one of the lake's many islands, where we would set up camp and spend the next two days fishing.

Our three boys -- Matt, 9, Brian, 7, and Sean, 4 -- were at the age where there was still a fine line between imagination and reality. So we fueled the adventure with stories of sea monsters and pirate treasure.

The island itself was not a long paddle away, but it took our little flotilla about an hour to reach it. Once there, Dawn and the kids began to unload the canoes while I pitched the tent on a knoll overlooking the shoreline.

Suddenly there was a shout from the direction of shore. Of course when you're on an island, any direction is toward shore. So I stood up, looked around, and finally saw Dawn waving at me. I waved back. "Love you, too, darling."

"The canoes, you idiot," she shouted. Sure enough, there were two canoes just like ours disappearing into the horizon. As a matter of fact they were ours. I made a dash for shore, but the canoes had drifted out of sight.

The boys, instead of unpacking, had been re-enacting one of Blackbeard's assaults on the British Navy. Brian and Sean had jumped from one canoe to another. Matt had attempted to repel the boarders when all three toppled into the water. That provided enough thrust to send the canoes, with our packs inside, to the middle of the lake.

We weighed our options. It was too far to swim after the canoes -- they were out of sight, anyway. We could have tried to signal a passing boat. But most of the boats on this lake traveled too fast and too far out to notice us. We had to wait for help to arrive.

We took stock of our provisions. We had the tent, some matches and a pocket knife. We'd be warm and dry, anyway. Our fishing rods and tackle boxes were ashore, too. With any luck we could catch something to eat.

I assigned the boys to firewood detail. I baited a hook and cast. While I waited for supper to nibble, I sat down, notched the end of a piece of driftwood to mark our first day, and made a mental entry into my journal.

"Day 1. Marooned. The kids, bless their little hearts, don't realize the seriousness of the situation. They cheered when I let it slip that we'd probably spend the rest of our lives here. That's what comes from watching too many reruns of Gilligan's Island.

"Dawn, too, seems to be down-playing the crisis. Maybe she's just being brave for the sake of the kids. Or maybe she's in the denial stage before true panic sets in. She said she refuses to let my melodramatics ruin another vacation.

"She's taking photos of everything as if this was a happy outing. That's okay. It's important to document this ordeal. Some day an archaeologist will find the camera among our bones and will develop the film to find out what happened. Maybe others will learn from our tragedy."

Soon I found myself pondering how many calories were in the three sunfish I'd caught. If we caught the same number each day, how long it would take before we starved to death? It was then that the boys stampeded into camp screaming for joy and doing a victory dance.

"Pirates!" shouted Matt.

"Three pirates with beards and swords!" shouted Brian.

"And drinking bottles of rum!" shouted Sean.

"But don't worry," Matt said. "We chased them away."

After Dawn and I calmed the boys, we were able to figure out that three fishermen had stopped on the other side of the island and were cleaning fish for a shore lunch. But these fishermen, our only hope of being rescued, made a hurried exit in their boat after our boys began to pelt them with stones and sharpened sticks.

"Those men weren't pirates. You should have told them we were stranded here," I told the boys.

"You always told us not to talk to strangers," they said.

I hung my head in despair and turned my attention toward cooking dinner. Survival manuals made it look so easy to cook without a frying pan. I wrapped the fish in large, wet leaves. Then I scooped hot coals on top of them so they'd bake. When the smoke cleared I couldn't distinguish the fish from the ashes.

The boys said they were full and didn't want any charred fish. I was so delirious with hunger that I imagined in the flickering light of the campfire that I saw peanut butter and jelly smeared on the boys' faces.

The next morning I realized that only some heroic act would get us off that island. I decided to build a boat. I quickly discovered the difficulty of trying to piece together birch bark. And it took until mid-afternoon just to carve out the letters "HMS Futility" on the side of the dugout canoe I started to make with my pocket knife.

Finally I realized that a simple raft might be best. I tied three logs together with the guy lines from the tent. It didn't look like much, but I found it would remain suspended about two feet below the surface with me sitting on it.

I waved a final farewell to Dawn and the kids and paddled away, my head and shoulders the only things above water.

Hours later, in the middle of the lake, exhausted and light-headed, my raft was at a standstill. I began to stab at the water with my makeshift paddle to ward off the sea monsters I imagined were closing in on me.

Then something grabbed me by the collar. I shrieked. But it was only Dawn and the kids. One of our canoes had drifted ashore just out of sight of our camp. The boys had found it the day before when I had sent them to look for firewood. They had opened our packs and feasted on peanut butter sandwiches after their victory over the pirates.

On the way home the boys said playing pirates seemed much more fun than playing wilderness survival. They asked if I could help them make bows and arrows so they'd be ready the next time they saw bearded men drinking rum.

Politics On
Little Stump Lake

(Originally published by Game & Fish Publications, October 1992)

"Who do you think is the best choice for president?"

My wife, Dawn, had warned me to avoid politics during the dinner conversation. But Jerome Thwarter, her new boss, didn't hunt or fish, so what was I supposed to talk about? Besides, he had brought up the topic. He had asked me the big question point blank.

I felt Dawn's future with the firm depended on my answer. And heaven knows we were having trouble supporting my hobbies on my income alone.

"President?" I swallowed hard. These days an outdoorsman had to have firm convictions about the issues. "'Loophole' Larry has his good points what with his legal background and all, but I think I'll vote for Ed Finicky. He's a banker and I think he'll do a better job keeping the club financially sound."

"No darling, you imbecile," Dawn said politely through gritted teeth. "I think Mr. Thwarter was referring to the upcoming election for president of the United States.

"Oh that. But the upcoming election at the Little Stump Lake Hunting and Fishing Club is much more interesting. You see, when Leo A. "President for Life" Minuscule got married recently to Maggie Piscatori, the club's vice president and perennial bass tourney champion, he decided it would be very presidential if they spent their honeymoon fishing in

Maine and then bird hunting in Texas.

"Since Leo and Maggie will be gone for some time, the club needs to elect an interim president."

"But don't you think it's important to discuss the national issues?" asked Thwarter.

"Of course. Finicky and Loophole discussed the issues in a debate last week. The election is scheduled Friday at the next club meeting. It will be poker night so we're sure to have a quorum."

"Yes, but what about the really important issues that affect us all," Thwarter insisted. "How about gun control?"

"Gun control is always a hot topic at the club," I said. "You have to consider not only the shooting position, but the sight picture, trigger pull, proper use of a sling, barrel length, stock configuration, handloads vs. factory ammo, lots of things."

"No, I'm talking about handguns."

"Loophole likes the Weaver stance, but Finicky insists on the old isosceles, especially when shooting the magnums."

"What about equal rights for women," Mrs. Thwarter chimed in.

"Women have always been involved in club activities. Maggie is a fine example of that. You won't find a better angler anywhere.

"Still, the question came up at the debate. Loophole said he has always worked to encourage women to join and participate. He claimed that thanks to him, women now had a permanent seat on the board.

"Finicky countered that Loophole's encouragement of women was the reason he was separated from his third wife. He said that the permanent seat on the board consisted of the new outhouse behind the club where we used to have the old maple tree.

"He reminded the voters that Loophole had suggested raising dues to pay for the new construction, but that it was Finicky himself who supported the pay-as-you-go method as being more fair.

"So you see there are a lot of similarities between the club election and the national race. Candidates still make the most of each other's personal scandals, accuse each other of wanting to raise taxes, and try to take credit for things they didn't do by playing word games."

The Thwarters barely spoke through the rest of dinner and Mrs. Thwarter, a vegetarian, didn't touch the stuffed grouse.

Still something positive came out of the discussion. I realized that in these times, with wildlife habitat being developed or ruined, and with growing, uneducated opposition to the outdoor sports, that it is more important than ever for the outdoorsman to become politically astute.

With that in mind, I've developed an outdoorsman's political handbook. In the book, soon to be available in water repellent nylon suitable for field use, I describe what the outdoorsman can do to educate would-be environmentalists on the importance of wildlife management and how to foster a positive image of the outdoor sports in the public eye.

I also include a chapter on running for office in your local rod and gun club, with suggestions on non-violent ways to resolve a deadlocked vote.

When the tally on Finicky and Loophole finished even, it was eventually agreed that the interim president would be the one who could break the most consecutive clay pigeons.

Unfortunately, Leo A. "President for Life" Minuscule left with the keys to the supply room, so the match can't take place until he returns, at which point the question of an interim president will be moot.

My book also includes a glossary of politcal terms. Following is a sample:

Caucuses: The escalation of yelps, clucks and gobbles as one turkey tries to woo the flock away from another turkey.

Trade Deficit: What you get when you swap a perfectly good shotgun for a boat that leaks.

Financing Covert Action: What you do when you donate to a pheasant-stocking program.

Lame Duck: Easily avoided by patterning your shotgun and knowing the limitations of steel shot.

Spending - Defense: You wouldn't believe the price I got it for and after all, guns are an investment, and it's not like I won't get a lot of use out of it, and I really need it for the type of hunting I'll be doing, and ...

Lobbying: The long process of standing in line to buy your hunting license because like everyone else you waited until the last minute.

Unemployment: An involuntary extended vacation you use to catch up on your hunting and fishing while avoiding pressing questions from your in-laws.

Two-Party System: Primary vote-getting technique. Finicky hosted a fundraiser, but lost votes when his guests found out there was a cash bar. Loophole hosted a party the next weekend and wrote the whole thing off as a necessary expense to be added to his legal retainer fee charged to the club.

As with national political candidates, he tried to get more votes by spending more money to look more generous to the people whose money he had just spent.

Bass Splashers
On The Air

(Originally published by Game & Fish Publications, June 1993)

I stood on the dock of the Little Stump Lake Marina, wearing the brand new shirt and ball cap that both shouted "Vern's Fishing Tackle Emporium" with huge red letters.

I carried a new Lyle Smugpuss Signature Rod and Reel Combo in one hand and in the other, a new Lyle Smugpuss Signature Tackle Box stuffed with new fishing lures, all compliments of Vern.

I had won a contest sponsored by Vern's shop and the grand prize was a day's fishing with Lyle Smugpuss, who was back in the area filming a segment for his weekly Bass Splashers television show.

I had fished with Lyle here once, long before all of his victories on the Bass Splashers tour, long before his television show and his personalized line of fishing tackle. I wondered if he would remember me.

"Stan, you old crankbait," Lyle said to me when he strode down the dock, his hand extended in greeting. "How have you been?"

"It's Steve. My name's Steve," I replied. "Gee you're looking good Lyle. How's the shoulder been holding up?"

"It's fine, but that isn't still on your mind after all these years, is it?" he said.

"Well, I felt bad because, well, I'm kind of the one who nudged you overboard reaching for the net when you hooked that lunker. When I went to fish you out I had no idea you could dislocate a shoulder so easily."

"Forget it, Stan. Besides, I don't think it would have hurt so bad if the arm hadn't been broken too. Really it was the best thing that ever happened to me. That was just before my first big Bass Splashers event, remember?

"I didn't think I'd be able to compete with my right arm and shoulder all wrapped up. I had to cast with my left hand for those three days, but I placed second.

"The media picked up the story, gave me a lot of good publicity and before I knew it I had several manufacturers on the phone begging to sponsor me on the tour."

"I guess it really was a lucky break, then," I said.

Lyle and I fished all day, with the Bass Splashers camera crew following closely in a second boat.

Six months later the episode was scheduled to be aired on television. I invited a couple of dozen people over for a party to celebrate my television debut.

"Hush. It's starting."

"Bass Splashers International presents, Fishing with Lyle Smugpuss with your host, three-time Bass Splashers champion Lyle Smugpuss."

We all hummed along to the theme song as we watched the opening segment showing Lyle catching bass all across the country.

"Welcome folks to another great Bass Splashers fishing adventure. I'm your host, Lyle Smugpuss. Today we travel to the very heart of Northern bass fishing waters: Little Stump Lake.

"My friend Stan and I got up early to take advantage of the great bass fishing this lake offers," Lyle narrated.

"Stan who?" Everyone in my living room seemed to say at once.

"Must be the wrong episode," Mike said.

"Can't be. They said Little Stump Lake," Floyd said.

"That Lyle," I said. "Such a kidder. He always calls me Stan. Look there I am in the boat with him, see?"

"Well that's the back of somebody's head," Ed said. "You sure that's you, Steve?"

"Dawn, tell the guys that's the back of my head," I said. "Surely you recognize the back of your own husband's head."

Dawn leaned closer to the television and studied the picture. "Well, I suppose it could be, but I'm not sure."

"Okay, stop joking around," I said. "Watch. You'll see."

The show focused on Lyle catching a couple of good sized largemouths, then broke to another commercial.

"Actually, I caught a couple of fish bigger than those," I said.

"Sure you did," Floyd said. "We haven't even seen that guy Stan catch a fish yet."

"I'm telling you I'm Stan. Stan is me. I'm the guy Lyle keeps calling Stan. Anyway they probably won't show the fish I caught because Lyle has some contractual agreement that no guest on the show can be seen catching a larger fish. It would detract from his expert status they said. Quiet. It's coming back on."

"Well, Stan, we've caught some good bass along this channel. Next I'd like to try out my new Whiplash rod near those wedbeds," Lyle said.

"Hey, I don't even see the back of your head now," John said. Where'd you go, Stan?"

"It's Steve. They put me ashore for a couple of minutes so the cameraman could get into the boat and get a better shot of Lyle heading the boat toward the wedbeds. They picked me up a couple of minutes later. Look there's my whole back this time. See I'm reeling one in. Oh that one pulled free. I remember that was a big fish, too."

"If all we're going to see is your back, then I want my shirt, cap and tackle back," Vern said.

"Oh, stop complaining Vern," Mike said. "Your shop got plenty of attention during the contest. You didn't really think they were going to give you free advertising on national television by doing a close-up of the front of Stan's cap and shirt did you?"

"It's Steve, remember?" I said. "Let's just watch the rest of the show."

"It's almost over now," Dawn said. "After this last commercial Lyle usually says farewell and gives a sneak preview of next week's show."

When the commercial ended it wasn't Lyle who came back on to say farewell.

"Steve, it's you," my guests shouted.

"With a full shot of my Vern's Fishing Tackle Emporium cap and shirt," beamed Vern.

"You didn't really think even an ego maniac like Lyle could keep me off screen the whole show, did you?" I said.

"Well, folks, that's all for this week," my television personae said. "I hope you enjoyed seeing all of the great bass fishing action on Little Stump Lake. It was a perfect day of bass fishing except for a little mishap at the end.

"But the crew here should be able to pop Lyle's shoulder back into place shortly. And to show you what a great athlete he is, Lyle will be back next week to show you how well he can cast that Whiplash rod with his left hand."

Eulogy
To A Pickup Truck

(Originally published by Game & Fish Publications, September 1993)

It was a dreary morning when a few of my closest friends and relatives gathered in my front yard to pay their last respects.

As I made my way to the front of the group, I was greeted with reassuring nods and comforting pats on the back. I was dressed in my best and only suit. Everyone else wore shorts and tee-shirts, except the Reverend Piddlebine, of course.

The Reverend read some words of inspiration, then bowed his head. I stepped forward, reached into my pocket and, with hands shaking, unfolded several sheets of paper.

"I would like to read this in honor of the deceased. The author, experiencing a similar loss, has expressed it much more eloquently than I ever could."

I was interrupted by the roar of an engine. Everyone turned to see Lou's Auto Recovery truck pull into my driveway, its huge tow boom mechanism looming like the Grim Reaper's scythe.

My wife, Dawn, quickly ushered the children inside so they wouldn't see. I cleared my throat and began to read aloud:

85

"Eulogy to a Pickup Truck

"I'll miss you my departed friend; who met a grim, untimely end.
  Not man, nor beast, just plain four-wheeler; I've sold my truck to a junk car dealer.

"What memories in your paint job pent; great tales afield in each scratch and dent. The time I fired at bird in flight; but didn't see you in my sight. Your coolant no more radiates; I splashed your grille with No. 8's.

"Upholstery mildewy, damp; no brakes upon the boat launch ramp. Up front did faithful canine ride; 'til joust with skunk did keep outside.

"In four-wheel drive each trail a cinch; with ready cash to hire a winch. Off road low limbs we often smacked; antenna bent and windshield cracked.

"Through shortcut had both axles buried; a time I wished I was not married. My spouse hiked long without good humor; though mauling bears were just a rumor.

"With gear piled high we traveled long; and never noticed what was wrong; until we stopped to buy some gas; then realized that underpass; we'd felt we'd made by skin of teeth; was much too low to squeeze beneath.

"Your cap had flipped into the road; and with it our entire load. Our tent, our packs and cooler, too; and somewhere yet was our canoe. Retraced our route, for miles were strewn; most every sort of jig and spoon.

86

"So many nights in back I spent; too stormy out to pitch a tent. Cold mornings rising from my bed; while hoisting pants I'd bump my head; then scramble to the driver's seat; with gaping holes beneath my feet. In need of heat, I'd beg you please; remember where I'd tossed my keys.

"To deer camp you would haul our gear; accumulating more each year. Forgotten heaps of junk surprising; I had no time for organizing.

"In headlight beam played cards all night; and lost my shirt in fading light. Next day I found your batt'ry drained; while not one hunting pal remained.

"I pushed you to the mountainside; Not quick enough to catch a ride.
You sped away with new-found zeal; and no one left behind the wheel. Since it was futile to cajole; I watched you turn cartwheel and roll.

"Your tailgate down great boasts I made; while game and fish there I displayed. The spike-horn buck, the trout though small; to you and me great trophies all.

"What cargo hauled in box now twisted; what chores performed 'cause wife insisted. Hauled wood to camp and trash to dump; hauled lumber home when wife said jump.

"Hauled groc'ries, toys, hauled bikes and bales; all sorts of things from antique sales. When work was done we'd hose you down; all ready for a night in town.

"I customized you, rig of mine; with rifle rack and scent of pine. Dry flies I stuck to visor felt; blue worms I left on dash to melt. A cushion brought the pedals nearer; a turkey beard

87

hung from the mirror.

"Suspension stiff, the ruts no factor; a comfort to my chiropractor. More power for those lofty summits; with pedal floored the gas gauge plummets. Explain to highway officers; of monster tires, speedometers.

"All shiny, new, just yesterday; how quickly you did fade away. Side mirrors gone, both doors are busted; flap with the breeze, completely rusted.

"Your frame is bent, your oil pan lost; a stump now wears your loud exhaust. Your hood's held down with length of twine; your brake pads squeal, your belts all whine.

"Your washers work, but wipers won't; your taillights do, but brake lights don't. Your shocks are shot and horn won't sound; odometer has turned twice 'round.

"Though fenders gone and bumpers hanging; windows cracked and pistons banging; transmission out and tires flat; to you my truck I tip my hat. Though each time out the odds I'd stack; you always got me there and back.

"And when they lifted you in tow; you pleaded, "Please don't let me go." Recalling all adventures shared; the tears poured out, emotions bared.

"I let you go with heavy guilt; the best truck that they ever built. And if I had it in my power; I'd bring you back this very hour; to joyously complete this rhyme; and take me hunting one more time."

Fighting
The Trade Deficit

(Originally published by Game & Fish Publications, March 1994)

"Dawn, great news. I quit my job!"

My wife sank into the nearest chair and covered her face with her hands in an attempt to hide her tears of joy. She wasn't one for ostentatious displays of emotion.

"I've got it all figured out," I continued. "We'll actually be further ahead if I hunt and fish full time."

I led her to the dining room table where I had spread all of our bills. I explained to her that most of our expenses were related to the fact that I was employed.

"See this is how much I make in a year. Subtract all of the taxes. Not much left. Then take out money for health insurance, the car payment, car insurance, gas, maintenance. Take out the cost of clothes and lunches and you see that I'm actually losing money by going to work.

"Now that I've quit my job, those expenses are gone. We can sell the car. The truck's paid off. Your paycheck will cover the house payment. What else do we need?"

"How about food?"

"Since I'll be a fulltime outdoorsman, I'll be bringing home lots more game and fish. I've also borrowed the Baker's roto-tiller. Look out back. Our yard is now one huge garden."

Dawn hung her head.

"Don't worry," I said. "Think of all the vegetables. Gardens are a lot of work, but it all balances out because I won't have

89

to mow the lawn anymore. Couldn't if I wanted to. I traded the lawn mower for these packets of seeds."

"Magic beans, I hope."

"You worry too much. Still, all of this won't make us completely self-sufficient. I might have to supplement by doing some odd jobs."

"Every job you've ever had has been odd."

"This will work, you'll see. Other things we need we can get through the old barter and trade system. You know, just like the mountain men used to trade their furs for supplies so they could go out and get more furs."

"We don't have any furs. Besides, the I.R.S. will get upset when you report one deer hide, two squirrel tails, and three brown trout as income."

"That was just an example. Trading the lawn mower for the seeds was just a start. The key is to always trade up. Look at this. I traded one of my old shotguns to Lenny for this great fly rod. It's a beauty, don't you think?"

"Yes. And I thought so three years ago when I bought it for you. How Lenny got it I don't know. You traded it to Dave for a bait-casting outfit that you later traded to Bill for that old tackle box."

"The tackle box, that's right, the one I lent to your brother, Floyd, and haven't seen since. See how it works? We don't need money. Everyone swaps for what he needs at that particular time. I didn't need that fly rod when you first bought it for me. But now it'll come in handy."

At dinner, Dawn suggested more cost-cutting measures.

"All you really need is one shotgun, one centerfire rifle, one rimfire .22 and maybe a couple of fishing rods. The rest you can sell to pay the bills."

I almost choked on the steak I was eating.

"Are you crazy? If I'm hunting and fishing full time, I'll need more equipment than ever. Even the older equipment I'll have to keep in stock for trading purposes. Why don't we

90

sell the living room furniture instead?"

Dawn pointed out that if I really wanted this change in lifestyle, I'd have to be willing to make some sacrifices.

"Take that steak you're eating for instance," she said.

"It's great, Hon. I don't know how you do it, but..."

"The deferred payment plan," she said. "I bartered the steak, no money down, from the Taylors who run the grocery store. But you have to chop their firewood until 2023."

So facing the alternative of having to chop firewood the rest of my life, I reluctantly agreed to sell some of my outdoor gear. Besides, after Dawn went to work the next morning, I tried pushing the old living room sofa through the front door. It wouldn't budge. The house must have been built around it. There was no way I'd be able to sell it unless I chopped it up and sold it for kindling.

In the evening I showed Dawn the display of outdoor gear in the garage, all set for my End of Employment Clearance Sale.

"See all the sacrifices I'm making?"

"These chest waders aren't yours," she said. "They belong to Kyle. That bowhunting target is Mike's, the bore-sighter is Tom's. Honey, none of these things are yours. They're all things you've borrowed."

She was right. I couldn't in good conscience sell or trade equipment that belonged to my friends. Besides, if Kyle or Mike or Tom showed up at my garage sale, I wouldn't get as far as an opossum crossing the road.

I needed another plan. I telephoned all of my friends and had them assemble at my house for an emergency meeting.

"I'm proud to announce the opening of my new business, Trading Post Resources, Inc. Let's face it. At one time or another, all of your hunting and fishing equipment ends up in my garage." Heads all nodded in agreement.

"All of you except me have fulltime jobs. That makes it impossible to afford all the gear you want or use all the gear you have. Under my plan, you will give me all of your hunting and fishing gear as usual. But now, for a modest fee, I will store and maintain all of the gear and loan it out library fashion to those on our membership list. Dawn will keep track of everything on her computer.

"You'll never have to worry about your wives' reactions to buying more stuff, since you can bring it directly here and they'll never know you spent the money."

Soon my business was booming. Each day my friends would line up in front of my garage.

"I need a good over-and-under for a trap shoot next weekend. Can I borrow one?" Fred asked.

Dawn checked the inventory. "All of our shotguns are on loan, but I can put you on a waiting list, Fred."

"But that over-and-under is my shotgun. Can't I borrow my own shotgun?"

"Here, Fred," I said. "Why don't you borrow this trolling motor and go fishing instead? Who's next?"

"I don't have any place to keep this old johnboat," Sam said. "How much will it cost to store it here?"

"Twenty dollars," I said, "with the understanding that we can loan it out. Just haul it to that dirt spot in my backyard where the veggies never came up. Bad seeds. On the other hand, Fred might want the boat to go with the trolling motor he just borrowed. He's going fishing next weekend. I'd love to go, but I never get to go hunting or fishing anymore. I'm tied up borrowing and lending equipment full time."

All About Muzzleloaders

(Originally published by Game & Fish Publications, October 2004)

"Life is like a muzzleloader," Vern said. "You only get one shot, so you stuff as much into it as you can and hope you get a real bang out of it."

"No, no, no," Morgan countered. "Owning a muzzleloader is like being in love. At first there's that special spark, but when the smoke clears and you can see things the way they really are. You realize she's the ramrod who views you as just another slug."

Morgan had been a marriage counselor, but was a little bitter after his third marriage fell apart.

I had stopped in to Vern's Gun Shop, Pizzeria, and Fishing Tackle Emporium to take a look at muzzle-loading black powder rifles. But the unsolicited advice I was getting from the usual crew of loitering, gun shop philosophers at Vern's was confusing.

"Both of you are wrong," old Doc Ferguson said. Doc was a retired pediatrician. He stepped forward, a shaky hand on a cane tapping and testing the rough wooden floor boards as if he suspected they might not support all of his 130 pounds.

"Owning a muzzleloader is like raising a young child," he said. "At first you're excited about having it. You soon learn, however, that it makes way too much noise and that no matter what kind of powder you use, it still emits an awful odor. It's a lot of work. You spend most of your time trying to keep it clean. And once you've had it a few years, you find you hardly ever take it out to play anymore."

"You're close to it, Doc," Frank chimed in. "But buying a muzzleloader is more like buying an economy car." Yes, Frank had been a car salesman. Now retired, he spent his time hanging out at Vern's, still trying to advise people on how they should spend their money.

"Just like an economy car," he said, "you think you're getting a bargain, but after you add up all the accessories you want and need, you find you've spent more than you originally intended. It's no longer a bargain.

"At first you're proud to show it off. But after you've put a few scratches on it, you've drastically reduced its resale value. And like Doc was getting at, it's the maintenance that really gets you."

I'd always been reluctant to get involved with muzzleloaders. I already had lots of hobbies and lately not enough time to devote to any of them. Why did I need one more? I had guns I rarely fired, my canoe in the garage had become merely a storage container for my dust-covered fishing tackle, and my hiking boots had set up a permanent camp somewhere in the back of my closet.

"Cleaning guns is drudgery," Morgan said, "and with a muzzleloader, you spend more time cleaning it than shooting it."

"It's not that bad," Vern said.

"Why bother with separate components when it's so easy to buy a box of cartridges to fire in a modern firearm?" Frank said.

"Why do I bother having this shop," Vern said, "when you guys always try to talk my customers out of buying anything?"

"With muzzleloaders, it takes longer to get over the disappointment of a missed shot," Doc said. "I'd stand there at the range being forced to think about it the whole slow time

I'd be reloading. With modern firearms, I can redeem myself right away by firing another round. Hit paper with a quick follow-up shot and you forget all about the miss."

"It's the other way around," Vern told me. "You have fewer misses with a muzzleloader because you take fewer shots. Say you take two shots with a muzzleloader. You might miss one. In that same amount of time, you might take ten shots with a cartridge gun and miss five."

"You're missing 50% of your shots either way," Frank said.

"Don't think of percentages," Vern told me. "After those two shots with the muzzleloader, you can brag that with all the shots you took, you only missed once. You can show off the target and not lie because you literally fired a one-hole group, with one called flyer of course."

"I thought that if I ever decided to buy a muzzleloader, I'd go the full traditional route," I said. "I'd get a sleek, long-barreled flintlock rifle with a fancy wooden stock. I'd dress in buckskin from head to toe, you know, the whole Davy Crockett look."

"Traditional would be a good way to go," Vern said. "It'd make you appreciate the way things were. You'd be carrying a piece of history with you. You'd think of how we won our independence from the British, how we explored the frontier, how we defended the Alamo."

"Don't get too caught up in that fantasy," Morgan said. "The chances that the British would ever try to retake the colonies in your lifetime are remote. In the woods, the Red Coats you'd be seeing wouldn't be marching to fife and drum. They'd be other hunters."

"Yeah," Doc said, "and think of the enemy storming the walls of the Alamo while you're standing there helpless, not having enough time to reload."

"It sounds like you were there, Doc," Frank said.

"He could have been," Vern said. "He's old enough."

"Old enough to know better," Doc said. "I'd advise against

a muzzleloader that you'd probably take deer hunting only one or two days a year. Heck, I'll give you mine. I never use the darned thing."

"Doc, Morgan, Frank, the pizza's on me," Vern said. "Just take it over to the dining area and let my paying customers make up their own minds."

"Thought you'd never offer," Morgan said.

"We have a deal then," Frank said.

"Some dining area," Doc said in a huff. "We'll have to clear the bait canisters off of Vern's reloading bench."

The muzzleloaders I was handling at Vern's weren't the traditional variety. These new guns had short barrels, perfect for hunting at close range in thick cover. They had weather-proof synthetic stocks and dependable in-line ignitions with shotgun primers. They sported bright fiber optic sights that even I could see without a magnifying glass.

Once the old-timers were gumming their pizza in the corner, Vern was free to launch his sales pitch. When he had finished, I had thumbed my nose at tradition and had purchased a modern, in-line muzzleloader.

The whole thing was much easier than I had expected. I had no powder to measure; all I had to do was drop in a couple of pellets. Cleanup was easy too. I'd unscrew the breech plug, put the muzzle in a bucket of hot soapy water and run a swab through with a cleaning rod. I have so much fun shooting it, I use it much more than one or two days a year.

Contrary to the wisdom of the old-timers, I found that owning a muzzleloader was more like owning an old gun dog. It might be a little slower to get into action, but it'll get the job done, will bark a lot less, and will likely become your sentimental favorite.

Getting Bugged About Walter

(Originally published by Game & Fish Publications, August 1993)

Walter was starting to bug me. He was bent over, knee-deep in the river, scooping up insects. It was the same on all of our backcountry fishing trips. He spent more time fishing for bugs than fishing for trout.

"It's crucial that I use the most appropriate caddis fly imitation," he said.

I, on the other hand, had no trouble locating bugs.

"How about the old Culex Pipiens," I suggested.

"The Culex what?"

"The Culex Pipiens. That's the genus and species of the common mosquito. While you've been trying to match the hatch, about five billion blood-craving mosquitoes have decided to siphon me dry."

Walter looked up to see me slapping and clapping at the mosquitoes as they attacked every inch of my flesh. He instinctively started humming, "Head, Shoulders, Knees and Toes, Knees and Toes."

"Now that you mention it, I do see a few," he said. Sometime during Walter's childhood, his brain had come to two roads diverging in a wood, and instead of taking the one less traveled, it had stepped off the trail completely.

"A few? That's not a metaphorical dark cloud hanging over my head," I said frantically. "Those are bugs. They're probably breeding in that bog over there. And I forgot my repellant. Let's get out of here. Maybe we can find a spot to camp downstream with fewer bugs."

Walter and his retriever, Decoy, climbed into the front of the canoe. I took off my shoes, waded out a few steps, gave the canoe a shove, then hopped aboard.
Walter reached into his pack and handed me a bottle of some perfumed skin lotion that was reputed to repel bugs.

Walter couldn't have been using this stuff himself. It was the first day of our week-long canoe trip and he already smelled faintly as if he had rolled in the same stuff Decoy had found in the bog. The bugs seemed to be staying away from him.

A bee buzzed by, caught the sweet fragrance of the lotion and wasted no time summoning his co-workers.

"That's the one trouble with that stuff," Walter said.

I ducked and dodged to keep from being pollinated. Decoy thought he would help. He lunged at one and snapped his jaws. The canoe tipped and we almost capsized. With a few panic-powered strokes of the paddle, however, we outdistanced the bees.

I had no time for relief. Suddenly I felt a stabbing pain in the little toe of my right foot. I looked and saw a deer fly dining happily. I swatted him with my ball cap, but too late. My little toe was now swollen bigger than my big toe.

Downstream the shoreline opened flat and wide, a perfect place to camp. Walter resumed his hunt for the caddis fly. He was in a world of his own, a world that obviously did not include insects. They hadn't bothered him at all. Back in my world, somewhere in the neighborhood of reality, there were now black flies.

I threw a series of left jabs and right hooks into the cloud of bugs, but I was caught by a flurry.

"You look like you've just gone a couple of rounds with Mike Tyson," Walter said.

I looked at my reflection in the water. My face and hands

98

were covered with bites. One eye was nearly swollen shut. I hobbled back to camp, one shoe on, one shoe off due to the swollen toe. Walter dug into his pack again and this time handed me a camo headnet he usually used for turkey hunting. It was like closing the barn door after the horse was gone, but I was still grateful.

We started a good, smoky campfire, an overrated insect repellant since it always chokes you, stings your eyes, and forces you to retreat with the bugs. I sat on a log with my traditional plate of beans and listened to Walter as he tried to cheer me up.

"Do you know there are about 800,000 species of insects?" he said.

"I'm sure I've been assaulted by at least that many today," I said.

I shoveled a spoonful of beans and realized too late that I should have lifted the headnet off my face first. Some of the beans spilled onto my shoeless foot and were immediately out-flanked by several platoons of ants, the same kind I saw on a television documentary, I thought, that are capable of devouring an entire musk oxen.

"Most of the species are harmless," Walter continued. "Some are even beneficial to man."

I looked at the strange bumps on my arms and tried to recall the symptoms of malaria and yellow fever. I thought of Lyme Disease and began to look for ticks.

"Some places you don't have to worry about mosquitoes," Walter said. "Bats keep the insect populations down."

Great, I thought. Then I'd have to worry about rabies instead of Eastern Equine Encephalitis and the West Nile Virus. Decoy sat down next to me and began to scratch. Even man's best friend carried a supply of insects in case you needed extras. Fleas on rats carried the black plague, didn't they?

"Some people have to be careful, though," Walter said.

"They have allergic reactions to bites. Their throats swell until they can't breathe."

I reached to check my own throat and spooked the large black spider that had been perched on my collar. I dropped the plate of beans and ripped off my shirt.

"Fire too hot?" Walter asked.

"Walter, what's that they say about the venom of a black widow spider compared to that of a rattlesnake? I need to know."

"Technically," Walter said. "Spiders aren't classified as insects."

"Oh well, then I have nothing to worry about, do I?"

"Why are you getting so irritated?" Walter asked. "You know, I've heard that some animals are driven completely loco by pestering insects."

I sat back down on the log and stared at the fire. A moth fluttered, then nose-dived into the flames. Ha! One down, how many billions to go? I looked at Walter.

"Walter, tell me," I said through gritted teeth. "Why is it that you haven't been bothered at all today by mosquitoes, black flies, gnats, no-see-ums, bees, fleas, ants, anything?"

"Because I smeared on this bear grease preparation before we left." He must have sensed my hostility because he inched his way down the log away from me.

"Bear grease?" I asked.

"Yeah. Same concoction the pioneers used a century and a half ago. Smells really bad, but it works. Simple recipe, actually. All you do is take one grizzly bear, a cup of vinegar, a..."

"Stop it, I've had enough!" I lunged for Walter's throat. "It's not the insects that are driving me loco, Walter, it's you! I hate you, Walter! I hate your caddis flies, I hate your bear grease, and I hate your flea-ridden dog!"

I collected my senses, released my strangle-hold on Walter, and went back to staring at the fire as if nothing had happened.

"Gee," Walter said, amazed at my outburst. "I had no idea you felt that way. We can leave Decoy home next time, no problem."

I apologized to Walter. That night a lone mosquito periodically interrupted my fitful dreams of earwigs chewing brain cells and giant insects destroying Tokyo. When I sensed the mosquito was close, I'd slap the side of my head to replace the bug's humming with a hypnotic ringing in my ears. That was one fishing trip that didn't end too soon.

"I'm glad you're home," my wife, Dawn, said. She was preparing a list of chores. "First, can you take care of that wasp's nest in the attic? It's too high for me to reach."

How To Make Fish Chowder

(Originally published by Game & Fish Publications, July 1993)

A while back I received a message in a bottle from a distressed reader who wrote:

"Dear Parting Line: I'm a strong advocate of catch and release, but from time to time I do wish to keep my catch. Can you provide any insights on the best ways to prepare fish?

"P.S. I'm marooned on a remote island with no provisions. Could you please forward my coordinates to the nearest Coast Guard vessel?"

Dear Marooned: When catch and release became a fishing norm, millions of fisherman secretly breathed a sigh of relief.

The practice has enabled fisherman to retain their favorite part of the recreation -- catching fish -- while allowing them a socially acceptable way of avoiding the most dreaded part of fishing: cleaning and preparing fish for the table.

Still there are those who deep in their twisted subconscious believe they must somehow punish themselves to alleviate the guilt they feel from going fishing instead of staying home to scrape the old paint off their window trim. Those are the ones who insist on keeping their catch, and even eating it.

Let's face it. There are a limited number of useful things that can be done with a fish out of water. Once they stop flipping around they quickly lose their entertainment value. They make terrible gifts to the woman in your life and I discovered as a boy that they ride somewhat uncomfortably in

your pants pockets.

The longer you keep them around, especially on hot summer days, the fewer social invitations you'll receive.

Since I've found it more challenging over the years to fish for the smaller species, I've often sifted them into my aquarium with the hope that my guppies wouldn't eat them.

It would be wasteful to throw them away and sometimes releasing them back into the water would negate the effort you put into catching them, especially if you're like me and your catches are few and far between.

When that first brave fisherman snagged, speared, netted or otherwise landed his first fish thousands of years ago, he was faced with the same question: what do I do with it now?

I remember fishing for perch and sunfish with a friend when I was about 12 years old. Each fish we caught we threw onto the bank behind us.

After a while we looked back to see how our catch was adding up. To our amazement all the fish were gone and in their place was my friend's Labrador retriever, sitting on the bank panting and thumping his tail.

That first primitive fisherman probably disposed of his first catch the same way. He probably acted on instinct, seeing no other practical purpose to the scaly, slimy, ugly creature, and simply stuffed it into his mouth and swallowed it raw.

That scenario gives credence to scientific theories reasoning that early man subsisted on and actually preferred to eat fungi, tree bark and the decaying remains of unfortunate animals trampled in wooly mammoth stampedes.

Today if you eat raw fish you're in danger of being labeled either an uneducated savage or a cultured, pretentious upper-class snob, depending of course on the tableware, if any, employed in the consumption process.

For those who insist on keeping their catches, but who decline to dine the fashionable way on raw fish like my friend's Labrador retriever, there is still hope. The answer is my recipe for fish chowder.

The first step is to preserve the flavor of the fish from the moment you set the hook. Lean overboard and swish you hands through the water to rinse away any excess worm bedding material. Wipe your hands off on your jeans.

Handle the fish carefully to avoid contaminating its flavor with any of your blood drawn from an untimely jab by a hook or dorsal fin spine.

Throw the fish into your cooler with the half-melted muddy ice, leftover lunch and any unfinished beverage of your choice. Allow to marinate until you get home, stirring often. Wipe your hands off on your jeans.

As soon as you get home put a kettle of vegetables on the stove to boil. However you decide to prepare the fish, believe me it will end up as chowder so you might as well get the veggies started.

Don't waste a lot of time cleaning or filleting the fish. By the time you're through hacking away, be-heading, de-finning, de-scaling and otherwise studying the anatomy of your catch, there won't be enough to bother with anyway.

You can cook your fish prior to putting it into the kettle, but this too can be a waste of time. If you grill it, the half-charred, half-raw remainder of what didn't fall into the coals will be less than appetizing, unless you're camping, in which case the primitive fisherman instinct takes over and you'll eat it rather than take the time to gather fungi and tree bark for dinner.

Frying is no better. But if you do decide to fry, roll the fish in bread crumbs first. That way the burnt portion you end up scraping off will be mostly breading and you'll keep fish loss to a minimum.

The only way I find the taste of my fried fish satisfactory is when I fry it in bacon grease. That's because I like bacon and, as you know, anything cooked in bacon grease ends up tasting like bacon.

Whether you decide to grill, broil, bake or fry, take the remaining unidentifiable fish substance, which now should have the consistency of corned beef hash, pick out any remaining bones, and toss it into your kettle of boiling vegetables. Then wipe your hands off on your jeans.

Follow this recipe and you'll have perfect chowder every time. Quantities of the various ingredients are unimportant since no matter how much you make, it will only serve two: your Labrador retriever and yourself.

How To Fish
A Stream

(Originally published by Game & Fish Publications, April 1997)

Fishing streams for trout -- especially on opening day -- is for grownups. At least that's what I was trying to convince my three boys.

"It's not like sitting on the dock at the lake and plopping a bobber into the water," I said. "It takes skill, a careful approach, precise casting, and patience, lots of patience. You'd get bored just standing there and you probably wouldn't catch anything except a cold. There will be other times."

"What about your cold, Dad?" asked Sean, my youngest son. "I heard you coughing into the telephone and telling that mean son-of-a-boss guy that you couldn't go to work today."

"You dummy, Sean," said Brian, my middle son. "When you're a dad you can go fishin' any time you want. You don't even need a note from Mom."

I finally consented to let my oldest son, Matt, go with me. He was 14, and a good age, I figured, to start carrying all of my heavy stuff.

"Should we bring the chest waders or hip waders?" Matt asked as we packed the car.

"It doesn't matter," I said. "The first principle of stream fishing states that a fisherman will always wade out to approximately two inches over his waders, no matter what kind he uses.

"On second thought," I considered, "we'd better go with the hip waders. The water's like ice this time of year and with the hip waders we'll have a shorter swim back to solid footing."

There were a few snowflakes shivering through the air that opening day, but it didn't keep the anglers away from Willow Creek. There were cars lined up for a couple of miles along the best access road.

"Hey, look, there's Uncle Floyd," Matt shouted.
Sure enough, there was my enterprising, but unemployed brother-in-law unloading the back of my old pickup truck. I still considered it mine since he had yet to pay me for it.

"Out for a little fishing, Floyd?" I asked.

"No," he said, eyeing our rods and tackle boxes. "You'd have to be crazy to fish here opening day. It's strictly business for me."

He unrolled a sign that read, "Floyd's Mobile Creekside Cafe."

"Wait until the aroma of my fresh, hot coffee starts wafting downstream," he said. "Those chilled-to-the-bone anglers will be lining up over here. I've got all kinds of baked goods, too -- donuts, pastries, you name it. Want to stay and help me, Matt? Share in the profits?"

"No thanks, Uncle Floyd," my son said. "You still owe me ten dollars from last winter on the lake when I helped you with 'Floyd's Ice Shanty Hot Dog Stand.'"

"You couldn't cut the mustard that day," Floyd said, shaking his head. "I don't think I owe you a thing."

"Nobody could cut the mustard," Matt said. "There was a wind chill factor of 30 below. We froze more than our buns that day."

"Okay, I'll tell you what," Floyd said. "How about double or nothing? Stay here, help me and get your dad to chip in 20 dollars for more plastic coffee cup lids and, depending on how we do today, I'll double what I owe you. Or you can opt for nothing, because that's what they're catching on Willow

108

Creek today."

Matt politely declined the business opportunity and walked ahead toward the creek while I paid Floyd 20 dollars for the guarantee that there would be no anonymous calls to my office reporting my suddenly improved health.

Matt soon learned the second principle of stream fishing: Every opening day, it's as if someone has struck gold on all of the good trout streams; the competition for the best pools is intense.

"This place is packed, Dad," Matt said. "Where are we going to fish?"

"Relax, Son. This elbow-to-elbow opening day ritual is what helps to foster that special camaraderie among fishermen."

Ten minutes after we arrived, the fight broke out. Someone took someone else's spot, cast across someone's fishing line, or remarked on the facial similarities between the trout and someone's mother. I don't recall how it started and it's not important.

What is important is that I didn't want my impressionable son to witness the melee, so we left.

"I want you to understand, Matt, that not all fishermen are like that," I said as we pulled the car over to let the police cars rush past.

"I know," Matt said. "Not all fishermen are that big. I couldn't believe you called him a ..."

"Never mind and don't repeat it," I said.

"Anyway, it was cool after he hit you and you fell into the next guy, who fell in to the next guy and they all started fighting in the mud. Can you see out of that eye at all, Dad?"

The next stream we tried wasn't nearly as crowded. We stood on one bank and snagged our line repeatedly in brush on the opposite bank.

"Let me guess," Matt said. "The third principle of fishing streams is that the width of a stream is usually less than the length of your cast."

"Now you're catching on."

I also taught Matt that the fourth principle of fishing streams states that, normally, the largest fish will be holding in a part of the stream that is the most inaccessible from your approach.

"You could use that to your advantage to locate fish, except that the fifth principle states that after you painstakingly navigate the most circuitous route to that spot, you'll suddenly look up to find another fisherman has made his way to the very spot ahead of you."

On the way home, I touched upon the sixth principle pertaining to the natural attraction between overhanging branches and fishermen drifting in canoes.

When we got home, I went straight upstairs to soak in a hot bathtub. I felt a real cold coming on. Matt went into the kitchen to get some ice for my eye and found his mom eating pastry at the counter.

"Your Uncle Floyd was here a little while ago," she said. "He was selling baked goods for some charity. You could learn a lesson from him on how to act more grown up. How'd you make out with your dad?"

Ready For Anything

(Originally published by Game & Fish Publications, May 2002)

I was in my car, on my way to work, waiting out a red light. I was adrift in the monotony of my everyday routine and found myself gently tapping my head against the driver's side window in rhythm to the knocking of the pistons.

"Must be low on oil -- probably three or four quarts," I thought. "I just checked it too, last, when was it? Probably last spring. I'll put it on my to-do list."

Then something in my head must have rattled briefly into alignment, allowing a brain wave to slip through and splash onto the desolate shore of my consciousness.

"It's not just my pistons that are knocking," I thought. "It's opportunity, and yes, buddy, I see that the light has turned green."

I thought about how much time we spend in our cars, going back and forth to work, running errands, hauling the kids everywhere. If we were prepared, I reasoned, maybe we could squeeze in some outdoor recreation between those tedious errands.

Since then, I've always carried what I call a "ready kit" in the trunk of my car. It consists of a large plastic storage tub with a cover.

In it I keep my outdoor basics: a couple of those fishing rods that pull apart into 1 1/2-foot sections for travel, a small box containing hooks, sinkers and a few versatile lures; a flashlight; a couple of plastic ponchos; a grill; a small frying pan; a small cook pot with cover; forks and spoons; matches in a watertight bag; a general purpose fixed blade knife; a couple of water bottles; a length of 1/4-inch rope; a box of .22 rimfire ammunition; hearing protectors; shooting glasses; and binoculars.

I usually store some canned food for an emergency, such as the time my wife, Dawn, found out how much I really paid for the last shotgun I bought, and I had to survive her cooling off period. It's not excessive to stock a week's provisions for such cases.

With my ready kit, I can leave for work a little earlier, come home a little later, and make slight detours on the way to do errands. That buys enough time for a little extra fishing or shooting that rarely becomes a topic of conversation at the dinner table.

"Boy, you should have seen the long checkout lines at the grocery store," usually covers it.

Sometimes the ready kit's a lifesaver. Take the time we went to visit Dawn's Great Auntie Matilda. We sat fidgeting around Auntie's kitchen table while she made tea and told us the behind-the-scenes details of her most recent surgery.

"I've got a great idea," I said. "What if I run down to that little store just over the bridge by that stream that looks like it might have some big trout in it," I said. I'll pick up some of those tasty little pastry cake things, you know, with the frosting on them, and I'll be right back."

"No need," Auntie said. "I made some gall stone cookies with cinnamon on top."

Okay, she didn't say "gall stone" cookies, but they looked like it, and having eaten there before, I knew they'd feel like it going down.

"Well then, I'd better get some more milk for the kids to drink," I said.

"I'll go to help him pick it out," my son Matt said.

"I'll go to help him carry it," my son Brian said.

"I'll go to make sure they don't get stuck in the magazine

aisle," my son Sean said.

"I'm staying here with Mom and Auntie," my daughter Stephanie said. Sometimes the young make all the sacrifices.

The contents of the ready kit can vary. If there's a chance for some turkey hunting, in goes the camo suit and a box call.

"Spring turkey season is the tricky one," I once explained to a new hunter, "but I'm an expert."

"You must get a bird every year, then," he presumed.

"Never shot one," I said. "The tricky part is getting a chance to go. Wives will grant you a few days to hunt in the fall. They will grudgingly let you go fishing in the summer, especially if you bring the kids.

"But tell them there's a special turkey hunting season in the spring and they'll cry foul. They'll do anything to stop you. I've been married 20 years. I know the moves like a chess master.

"First, if Dawn anticipates I'm getting ready to go turkey hunting, she'll find a list of chores to keep me occupied. I counter that move by simply delegating those same chores to the boys and promise them pizza and movies later.

"Next I have to disarm Dawn's security system. I'm not talking about electronic surveillance here. I'm talking about six-year-old Stephanie.

"Anytime I try to sneak out for some recreation, the alarm sounds: `Mom, I think Dad's going hunting again, and he didn't clean the garage yet.'

"Disarming the security system is easy too. All I need is a decoy.

"'I'll play a board game with her, but no dolls,' my son Sean confirmed as I handed him a five-dollar bribe.

"One time, I thought it was checkmate. As I was about to leave, I found Dawn had removed my camo suit from the ready kit.

"'I threw it in the wash,' she said. `It looked like it must have been in there for years.'

"It was,' I said. `What difference does that make?"

"I didn't concede," I told the new hunter. "I pulled the suit out of the wash and draped it across the dashboard with the defroster on high. If I hadn't run the car into that tree I would have made it."

A word of caution: sometimes having a ready kit can backfire.

"I haven't been fishing for years," my mother-in-law said as she got into the car. "Dawn had some things to do, and she said she knows you always carry an extra rod and reel in the trunk."

I repeatedly knocked my head against the driver's side window in time with the pistons.

My Mid-Life Crisis

(Originally published by Game & Fish Publications, August 1997)

I felt like a deer carcass that had been left out too long. I had been hanging in there, aging very nicely I thought, when suddenly, everything was spoiled. I had turned 40. It was a rotten thing. It stunk.

Dawn had invited a few friends over to the house to sling "old man" jokes at me in celebration of my impending senility.

"Everyone's in the backyard," she said to people as they arrived. "We thought the best way to cheer up a grumpy old outdoorsman would be to have a party outdoors."

"Oh, how nice," one guest said. "Everyone's gathered around a campfire."

"No," Dawn said. "Those are just the candles on Steve's cake. Matt, keep that fire extinguisher handy! We decorated the cake with a depiction of a fisherman snagging his line in a tree. I'll just have to remember to remove the hooks before we cut the cake."

Forty was like an overhanging tree branch. I didn't see it coming until it smacked me in the face.

"What happened to those last 20 years?" I asked Dawn.

"They slipped past when you were out hunting and fishing," she said. "While you were gone we had four kids and several thousand loads of laundry."

"But I'm 40 now. I'm starting to realize that I'm so far along on my trail in life that it's too late to turn back. I feel like I've taken so many unexpected turns that now I'm standing in the middle of nowhere with a boulder blocking my path as I wonder, 'How the heck did I get here?'"

"Many people at 40 are still in their prime," Dawn said.

"Prime candidate for a heart attack maybe," I said. "I should have started planning for my retirement years ago. I always wanted to spend my retirement hunting and fishing. But I've spent so much on hunting and fishing I don't know if we're going to be able to afford it now."

"It could be worse," Dawn said. "At least you chose activities you can do for a lifetime. Look at all of your ex-jock friends. They're trying to recapture their days of glory by twisting their knees in over-30 softball and basketball tournaments or by nearly killing themselves entering marathons."

"I forgot to tell you I signed up for that three-day, 90-mile canoe race coming up next month."

"I don't know why you guys always have to try to prove you can do things at 40 that you couldn't even do at 20."

"Because time is running out," I said. "I may never hunt lions in Africa, fish for salmon in Alaska, hunt moose in Canada. I may never climb Mount Rushmore."

"Don't you mean Mount Everest? Mount Rushmore is the one with the presidents."

"What does it matter? I'll never be president either."

"When did you ever want to be?"

"Never, but 20 years ago at least there was a remote possibility. Now that I'm 40, I know there are many things I'll never do whether I want to or not."

"So now you're worried that you can't do the things you don't want to do? Look, we all think you're just as good as ever. When you run around with the kids in the backyard, they think they're getting faster. They don't notice you're just slower because you've gained so much weight. And I think the way you comb your gray hair is an attractive way of covering your bald spot."

"You had to mention the bald spot. You know that's a sensitive area with me."

"Especially when you forget to put sun block on it during the summer," she said. "Look on the bright side. In a couple of years you'll be able to use your shiny pate to signal rescue planes."

I thought about it all through the cake and ice cream. I began to realize that for every negative aspect of being an "old" outdoorsman, there was a benefit to being what I prefer to call a seasoned veteran of the outdoors.

For instance, an outdoorsman knows he's over 40 when his prescription eyeglasses have greater magnification than his rifle scope or when, in order to use his binoculars, he first has to take off his bifocals.

The veteran outdoorsman, however, can use those bifocals as an emergency fire starter. He just has to be cautious walking through dry brush on sunny days that he doesn't start fires inadvertently.

Speaking of eyesight, an outdoorsman knows he's over 40 when, instead of having his iron sights lined up on the fuzzy, little rabbit, it always seems as if the rabbits are all lined up, but the iron sights are a little fuzzy.

The benefit for the veteran outdoorsman is that he can put away his rifle, take out his shotgun, and unleash the veteran beagle, who's also been putting on some extra pounds and probably needs to chase more rabbits.

An outdoorsman knows he's over 40 when he tears off a piece of venison jerky and his teeth come off with it. The benefit is that, to keep his teeth from chattering in the cold, the veteran outdoorsman can simply take them out and put them in his pocket.

An outdoorsman knows he's over 40 when he tries to buy a part for his favorite rifle and he's told they stopped making parts for it 15 years ago.

A veteran outdoorsman grasps this opportunity and buys a

117

new rifle, which will probably weigh less, shoot flatter, and may absorb some of the recoil of turning 40.

An outdoorsman knows he's over 40 when he starts forgetting things, such as his way home. A veteran outdoorsman is a master of excuses. When he forgets equipment, he's "traveling light." When he forgets his way, he's "taking time to appreciate nature."

An outdoorsman knows he's over 40 when he no longer stays out for hours stubbornly hoping that a fish will bite or a deer will come past his stand.

The veteran outdoorsman finds he's enjoyed himself just as much when he goes home empty-handed.

An outdoorsman knows he's over 40 when, the sapling he always stumbled over in the middle of the trail is no longer in the middle of the trail because the sapling is now a 60-foot maple tree and the trail goes around it.

The veteran outdoorsman knows that turning 40, like the maple tree, is just one more thing to wonder at before getting around it and continuing up the trail ahead.

Our Last Campout

(Originally published by Game & Fish Publications, September 1996)

My wife, Dawn, just picked up the photos from our last camping trip. All of our camping trips turn out pretty much the same, but she insists on documenting each one for all time anyway.

Here is the photo of our mini-van fully packed as we arrived at Ed's Shoreside Campground on Fawn Lake. Notice how everything is neatly lashed on the roof rack.

No, I had help from some guy in the rest area along the highway. I think that's him in the background of this photo of the seven-car pile-up that occurred roughly about the same time our lawn chairs went flying off the roof the second time. Here's a good one of me, but I think the trooper and the judge look much too serious.

Here is a photo of the kids standing next to the tent, and another of me setting up the tent, with one hand clutching a pole and the other tugging a guy line while trying to push in a stake with one foot.

It's deceiving. I guess from that angle it does look like the end of the pole is piercing the fabric of the tent, but I still think the wind blew some branch into it.

Here's our canoe loaded up for a day of fishing. It does look a little low in the water, now that you mention it. The kids had a great time. They got picked up by some nice family with a motorboat and spent the next three hours learning to water-ski.

That little speck bobbing in the water in this one? That's me swimming for shore. I try to get in a little exercise each day.

Here is a photo of our sons, Matt, Brian, and Sean holding up all of the fish they caught. See the fishing rod on the right, the one with the broken tip? If I didn't know better I'd say that was my new graphite rod, the expensive one I bought through the catalog. Dawn kept saying I must have set it down and left it somewhere.

And there's our baby daughter, Stephanie, over by the bait bucket, putting something in her mouth. That's me, of course, untangling a gob of line.

That's me again, heading off to collect firewood. There are the boys, gathered around the forest ranger, informing him of my last known direction of travel. Little Stephanie's sitting there. It looks like she's eating dirt.

Here's the family sitting together enjoying the warmth of the campfire. Yes, that's me with the singed eyebrows and soot on my face. I had blown on the embers to get the fire to flare up, and it did, before I had a chance to remove my face.

This photo shows the boys around the fire scorching three economy-sized bags of jumbo marshmallows. There's Stephanie, contesting a platoon of ants for a marshmallow that fell on the ground, and putting both marshmallow and platoon in her mouth.

Here I am using the only dry twig for miles that we didn't throw on the campfire to scrape a sticky glob of marshmallows off the bottom of my sneakers that had attracted a compost pile of dry leaves, along with two pennies, someone's old cigarette butt and the surviving ants that Stephanie didn't get a chance to eat.

The next photo shows the kids inside their sleeping bags cuddled close together, all sleeping like angels. What this photo doesn't show is the scuffle that preceded this scene because Matt didn't want to sleep next to Brian, who didn't want to sleep next to Sean, who wanted to sleep next to Mom, but not next to Dad because he always snores and because Stephanie just spit up on Dad's sleeping bag, which happened, Dawn figured, because Stephanie must be sensitive to the different brand of applesauce she ate for dinner.

Here I am being roused by the kids at 5 a.m. Note the puffy eyes, unshaven face and the few remaining strands of hair sticking out in all directions. This is how I will look, documented in photo albums for all time, for the amusement of my great grandchildren.

Here we are shopping in the Village of Fawn Lake. After roughing it for two days to get rid of the stresses of civilization, we were ready to tackle the bumper-to-bumper traffic, and throngs of pushing and shoving fellow vacationers in pursuit of souvenirs in the rows of tourist town shops along the narrow, crowded streets of Fawn Lake.

Here's a photo of the boys in their $25 Fawn Lake t-shirts, discounted at a season closeout ten percent. Each boy is

121

clutching a Fawn Lake pioneer commemorative slingshot. Each Fawn Lake pioneer commemorative slingshot has since been confiscated as part of the disciplinary process, much to the relief of neighbors and local songbirds alike.

Here I am sporting my new Fawn Lake ball cap with felt antlers coming out of the sides, holding my new, over-priced fishing rod in one hand, and a filled-to-capacity disposable diaper in the other because I can't find a trash can.

There's Stephanie, sharing an ice cream cone with some stray, one-eyed dog with patches of fur missing.

We're getting near the bottom of the stack now. Here I am packing the muddy tent away in the rain on the last day of the trip. I will set up the tent in my backyard to dry out when I get home on a day that it will also, undoubtedly, rain.

Here are the boys offering the family camping in the next site our entire supply of fish fillets that have been sloshing around all week in the cooler that I forgot needed ice.

Here are the boys holding up the same cooler, now filled with the toads, newts, grasshoppers, beetles, and other pets they accumulated over the week. Don't ask me how the one-eyed dog got in this photo.

Yes, Dawn did take a lot of photos on that campout. She slipped up, however, and put the camera down a couple of times. So, now that she's out of the room...

Here's a photo of Dawn trying to climb aboard an alligator-shaped float at the Fawn Lake Beach; another, documenting for all time, her standing in line outside the campground's women's showers; one, for the amusement of our great grandchildren, of her blowing her nose during her hay fever attack; another...

Weathering Opening Day

(Originally published by Game & Fish Publications, April 1998)

I fished through the closet of our guest room and came out with the bottom half of my lucky fishing rod.

"How did all my stuff get in here?" I asked my wife, Dawn. I continued to empty out the closet, searching.

"Since you're always out hunting and fishing, you're never here long enough to be granted full resident status," she said. "So I put your odds and ends in the guest room. Besides, you have so much junk, and the attic, basement and garage were full already."

"But tomorrow's opening day," I said. "How am I supposed to go fishing without the other half of my lucky fishing rod?"

"Lucky fishing rod? That's right, you did catch a fish with it once. Better forget about the fishing rod and bring along those winter boots and mittens instead. Have you noticed the weather? There's a blizzard outside."

It was true the weather was miserable. But weather was part of any outdoors experience and, after all, another definition of weather was "to endure bad things."

"If a guy's any sort of fisherman, he has to weather opening day weather," I said. "It's a tradition. You have to endure opening day."

"Since I married you, all I've had to do is endure," Dawn said. "Sometimes I think all you care about is trout."

"Opening day is not about trout," I said. "It's about being there."

The next morning, "being there" meant breaking the icy crust of the snow and sinking hip-deep with every step to the banks of Crazy Ned Brook.

The Crazy Ned flowed aggressively over its boulder-strewn bed and twisted and turned like an angry snake.

It was reputedly named after some old-time hermit who lived in the area more than a hundred years back, whose frozen body was found along the banks by some early season fisherman.

Then, as now, the pools of the Crazy Ned had a reputation for harboring large trout. When I made it to the edge of the brook, my lungs were heaving. I felt I was suffocating on chunks of cold air.

An old man was the only one fishing one of the better pools. He seemed unaffected by the weather, other than the fact that the fluffy snowflakes were accumulating on his overgrown gray eyebrows. Right away I dubbed him Crazy Ned.

"An-an-an-anything ni-ni-nibbling," I asked through chattering teeth.

"I hear they're really biting down at the reservoir," Crazy Ned said.

"Is-isn't the re-reservoir still fro-frozen?"

"That's right," he said. "They're still ice-fishing out there. Say, you know you're missing half of your fishing rod?"

"I had to bring it," I said. "It's my lucky rod."

"Lucky in that you found the half that holds the reel? I guess it doesn't matter much. Like I always say, it's not about catching trout. It's..."

"It's about being there," I finished for him. "I was telling my wife the same thing yesterday."

"You still have a wife? You must not do much fishing." The old man looked at me suspiciously. "My wife left me back in '68.

I wondered if he'd meant 1968 or 1868.

"It was terrible," he continued. "The weather that opening

day was worse than this. My rod was covered with ice and snapped in two on my backcast. I still have half of it around someplace, maybe stuffed in the closet of my guest room. I froze two fingers that day, too."

He held up a hand and the last two fingers of his woolen glove just flopped there. I shivered more from the story than from the cold.

The next few years I found Crazy Ned at the same pool each opening day. One year there had been a good thaw, so it wasn't the snow, but the run-off we had to deal with.

I looked at the torrent of muddy, churning water that was starting to flood the banks and knew I wasn't going to catch a trout that opening day either.

"I thought I had a bite just before you got here," Crazy Ned said. "But apparently I had merely hooked onto someone's barn that was being washed downstream."

Another opening day there was a relentless rainstorm. I looked down at my styrofoam cup of worms. The rain dribbled off the brim of my hat and the cup overflowed. My worms were drowned before they even got to the brook.

Crazy Ned was there, sitting on a stump. The rain made his long eyebrows droop even further. He looked like a shaggy dog peering out from under them.

To make matters worse, some kid was walking around with the grandfather of all trout. Fishermen in their rain suits and ponchos gathered around and stared at it to reinforce their faith that there were trout in the stream.

"Yep, it's a fish," Crazy Ned said. "I recognized it right away 'cause it's got fins."

I didn't need to look at the trout to believe there were fish in the brook. The fact that the old man was there year after year was good enough for me. Still, I suspected the kid had stolen the big trout from Johansen's Market up the street.

The next year, we had an unusually mild winter after a dry summer and things were drastically different. That opening day, the water was so low that everyone crowded around the remainder of what had been one of the deepest pools, nudging each other for elbow room.

I dumped my crispy worms into the dust and scooped out some water from the pool with my styrofoam cup.

"I'm going to take this water and fish over there where there's more room," I told the old man.

"Good idea," he said, "but don't you think you took a little more than your fair share?"

I held the cup up to eye level, nodded to the old man and poured a couple of teaspoons worth of water back into the mud puddle that had been the stream's best trout pool.

"That's more like it," he said.

Strong wind greeted us the following opening day. Small twigs and last autumn's leaves flew through the air. I had to hold onto my hat with one hand while I cast with the other.

"Wind's coming out of the west," Crazy Ned yelled above the gusts.

I looked at the old man, saw that his eyebrows were holding steady on a heading of due east, and nodded in agreement.

The following year was one of those rare opening days when the weather was perfect. I couldn't get the day off. As I got ready for work, I wondered if the old man had made it through the winter to celebrate this perfect opening day.

I looked in the mirror and noticed that as my hairline was receding, my eyebrows were getting longer. I would probably take the old man's place one day in the eyes of some younger fisherman.

"They'll be calling me Crazy Ned one day," I told Dawn. "I'll be the old man who always shows up on opening day, no matter what the weather. Except today."

Dawn tried to cheer me up.

"Keeping a job may not be about trout," she said. "But remember, collecting a paycheck is about being there, at least once in a while."

126

Hapless Harry's
Canadian Tragedy

(Originally published by Game & Fish Publications, February 1993)

When Hapless Harry Brighton walked into the lodge of the Little Stump Lake Hunting and Fishing Club everyone was eager to listen to his tale of hardship and woe.

Some members of the club tried to impress you with who they knew. In their futile attempts to gain credibility and status by association, they'd bore you by bragging of the feats of others.

"Believe me, I know a guy whose brother lives next door to the guy who caught the state record brown trout, so I know what I'm saying," was the typical, illogical argument for these guys.

But not for Harry. Harry's popularity grew because he was so imperfect, so human.

Nothing bonds people as securely as the minor mishap or trifling tragedy. This is especially true among those who hunt or fish. The small setbacks and little failures we all experience afield or afloat unite us and make for pleasant conversation besides.

Hapless Harry was the most likeable guy in the club because misfortune seemed to follow him wherever he went. If he hooked a trophy fish, his line would always snap just before he could net it. If he was bowhunting, he'd miss the 10-pointer because his arrow would be deflected by an unseen twig.

127

Through it all Harry would be smiling because, despite his misfortune, he always managed to be content with the mere effort.

Those of us at the Little Stump Lake club who relished in exchanging tales of hard luck could commiserate with Harry. The same things that had happened to all of us had happened to Harry, only more so.

So when Harry returned from the Canadian wilderness, we gathered around the table, prepared to shake our heads in empathy as he told his pitiable tale of the hunting trip of a lifetime gone sour.

"Well first I went to get on the plane," he said, "And you won't believe what happened."

"They didn't have your reservation?" "They lost your luggage?" "The plane was hijacked?" Everyone ventured a guess.

"No, nothing like that," Harry smiled. "I met this airline hostess. Apparently her folks knew my folks years ago. She recognized my name. Anyway, she's coming down for a few days during her next vacation."

"That's great Harry," I said. "But what about the hunting trip. Tell us what went wrong, er, what happened."

"Well we started out hunting moose along the west branch of the Upper Ubiquitous River, and..."

"Let me guess, the bugs were terrible?" "It rained the whole time?" "Found out too late there were Giardia in the water?"

"No, no. The guide pointed out a particularly remote area on the map and I..."

"You got lost?"

"No, I spotted this huge bull moose feeding along the river and..."

"You spooked him?" "Your gun jammed?' "Your scope fogged?"

"No. I shot him. My guide said it was the biggest one he's seen in several years along the Upper Ubiquitous."

By now everyone around the table was shifting uncomfortably and mumbling.

"Harry, you're saying everything went smoothly?"

"Guys, I'm telling you the hunting was great, the food was the best, everything was first class. We did run into a little trouble with bears, though.

"Ah ha!." Everyone's attention was piqued. "Bears ransacked the camp?" "Ate your moose?" "Mauled you?"

"Do I look like I've been mauled? Don't answer that. No. This enormous bruin came toward us rather quickly. Actually it was an all-out charge. My guide couldn't unsling his rifle in time. I stood my ground and managed to get off one hurried shot."

"And?" everyone said in unison.

"And he dropped dead not ten feet away from us," Harry said.

We all just stared in amazement. Some of the guys' mouths hung open wider than that of the mounted bass on the lodge wall.

"Of course that was just the first week of the trip," Harry continued. "Since I had filled my moose and bear permits, I spent the second week taking advantage of the best fishing I've ever experienced: pike as long as your leg and trout nearly every time I cast. Wait until you see the photos I took."

"Of course anyone could have a hunting trip like that if he's willing to shell out the big money," I said, eager now to find some drawback that could save Harry's reputation. "It must have cost you a fortune."

"It would have," Harry said. "But my moose and bear were so big and I caught so many fish that the guide said he'd give me a partial rebate if I agreed to let him use the footage of my trip in his new promotional video."

Now we were all depressed. We had all looked forward to a refreshing story of disaster. Instead, we now all envied Harry and his unbelievable luck.

"Great story, Harry." We slowly filed past him on the way out as if paying our final respects to a fallen comrade. "I'll never be able to afford a trip like that." "Some guys have all the luck."

On subsequent hunting trips Harry lost his hunting knife, dropped his sleeping bag in the lake, and even forgot his can opener. But no matter how hard he tried, he was never quite as human after that trip to Canada.

Hapless Harry retained a certain aloof celebrity status and the story of his Canadian hunting trip became a legend that was retold often, even by myself.

"Listen to me," I was caught saying more than once. "I know what I'm talking about. I personally know the guy who bagged the biggest moose ever recorded. And brave? He shot a charging grizzly at such close range that when it dropped, its tongue lay across the toe of this guy's boot. So don't tell me I don't know anything about hunting."

Hunting Memories
In The Attic

(Originally published by Game & Fish Publications, January 1998)

The cold air slapped my face and stung my lungs. I buttoned the top button on my hunting jacket and prepared for the climb ahead.

I trudged step over step, not really knowing what to expect. Then, there it was ahead of me -- the cluttered attic.

Had it been summer, no man could have survived more than an hour in the sweltering climate of my attic. But now, on a day that would have been perfect for rabbit hunting, my wife, Dawn, had issued a directive for me to cut a swath through this jungle of discarded household paraphernalia.

Without warning there was a terrific trembling in the floorboards. There was a great pounding on the stairs below me. I was directly in the path of the stampede -- Dawn had sent in the kids.

"Wow, look at all of this junk," Matt said.

"Can we keep this stuff?" Brian asked.

"It's already our stuff, Dummy," Matt replied.

"Let's play hide and seek," Sean said.

"Me help," Stephanie added.

It was apparent my guerrilla assault on the attic was about to turn into a major siege. There was no discipline in the horde. They charged ahead as if turned loose in a toy store after hours, with no clerk to throw them out.

Whenever you're faced with the colossal task of wading

131

through a lifetime of broken and abandoned belongings, the greatest pitfall is getting sidetracked down memory lane.

I stumbled into that very pitfall, when, only several layers into the accumulation, I found my old trunk of hunting equipment.

The kids gathered around as I brushed away the cobwebs. I worked the rusty latches and spoke the magic words. Well, in the excitement of opening an intriguing old trunk, they might have seemed to be magic words in a child's imagination.

Actually, I was muttering under my breath, wondering aloud about the time the dog and I were sprayed by the skunk, trying to remember whether I had burned those clothes or merely thrown them in this trunk.

I opened the lid and the hinges let out their requisite "creak." Immediately, four sets of little hands were digging through the contents.

"What's this old bone, Dad?" Sean asked.

"That's an antler from the first deer I ever shot," I said proudly.

"Isn't it kind of small for an antler, Dad?" asked Brian. "Anyway, where's the other one?"

"Mom told me," Matt said, "that after Dad shot the deer, he walked up to it and the deer suddenly got up. Dad was so surprised he fell over backwards and accidentally shot off the deer's other antler."

"You must be real good shot to hit something so tiny, Dad," Sean said.

"Tiny, Dad," Stephanie repeated.

"Look at this cool pocket knife," Brian said. "Can I have it, Dad?"

"I don't know why you'd want that old thing," I said. It looks a bit rusty and I think the tip of the blade is broken."

"Is that the one," Matt asked, "that you broke the time you fell in the lake retrieving a duck and you had to break into some guy's cabin to keep from freezing to death and you

132

had to live for three days on nothing but canned yams that you opened with this broken knife and then you almost got arrested?"

"No," I said. "I didn't almost get arrested. Once I explained..."

"What's a yam?" Sean interrupted.

"Me hungry, Daddy," Stephanie said.

"Besides," I said, "this is the knife I always used when I went grouse hunting."

"Oh, yeah, I remember now," Matt said. "That was the knife you used the time you locked your keys in the truck and you cut all the weather stripping from around the window to get inside and Mom yelled at you because the wind always whistled through after that."

"Look at all this film for your camera, Dad," Sean said. "Did you take lots of pictures on one of your hunting trips?"

"Yeah, I'll have to get those developed one of these days," I said and set the film aside.

"I'll bet it's from the trip where Dad spent all of that money to pay for a guide and went far away and all his friends at home shot deer and he didn't get anything," Brian said.

"Dad almost always gets his deer," Sean said. "Look here's a deer skin."

"Gross," Matt said when he unfolded it. "It's all moldy."

"All moldy," Stephanie said.

"Stephanie, where did you get that peanut butter sandwich?" Brian asked. "Yuck! Dad, I think she found it in the trunk."

"What are all those funny letters on that deer skin, Dad?" Sean asked.

"Those are there because Dad didn't get that deer when he was hunting," Matt said. "He got it on the way home from hunting. If you hold the hide in front of that old mirror over there, you'll see those letters spell 'Ford.'"

"I remember that old truck," Brian said. "Didn't the windows used to whistle?"

"Hey, Dad, what's this wire thing?" Sean asked.

"Be careful with that," I said. "It's an old piece of barbed wire."

"When Dad was hunting, he tried to duck under a fence and caught his pants on the barbed wire," Matt said. "Dad had to keep the piece of barbed wire to show his boss why he couldn't go to work because it would have been too embarrassing to show him the scar."

"Wow, look, a pirate gun!" Brian shouted.

"Hey, it's my old muzzleloader," I said. "I haven't seen that since..."

"Since you put that peek-a-boo hole in the back of the garage, right, Dad?" Sean asked.

"Yeah, and Mom hid the gun up here because she knew you'd never find it since you never get around to cleaning the attic," Matt said.

"Never clean," Stephanie said.

"Anyway, I can't wait until I can go hunting because you get to have all this neat stuff," Sean said.

"Yeah," Brian and Matt said together.

"Me too," Stephanie said.

The door opened below us.

"Hurry up guys," Dawn shouted up the stairs. "We're cleaning out the basement next."

Campfire
Ghost Stories

(Originally published by Game & Fish Publications, August 1998)

It was not a dark and stormy night. The rain had come earlier, while we had been fishing on Kleigmeier Lake.

"No sense in trying to catch any fish today," I quipped. "They'd only get wet out here like everything else."

No one was listening to my jokes. Dawn had passed out cups to our four kids and had made a game out of bailing the canoes.

"Quicker, children!" she screamed. "The water's getting deeper and I can't see the shoreline anymore!"

The evening had turned out much nicer. We hung our ponchos and other wet things from lines strung tree-to-tree around our campsite.

The kids hovered around the campfire skewering and torching marshmallows and arguing about who had eaten more.

Dawn sat swatting mosquitoes, her gaze fixed on the fire as she muttered over and over in her own sentimental way how this was definitely the last fishing trip she would ever take.

One of my boots was propped over the fire to dry. I poked the embers with a stick trying to find the other one, expecting to find a piece of smoldering sole or a bit of charred bootlace.

Every so often I looked over my shoulder into the darkness. The night creatures had begun to stir and I was alerted to every minute sound.

"No need to worry," I tried to reassure myself. Camping on the shore of Kleigmeier Lake had made me nervous since I had been a kid.

"Hey, Dad, do you know any ghost stories?" Brian asked.

"Well, I don't know if they're just stories," I said. "I suppose you boys are old enough to know the truth."

"If you're going to frighten the children, I'm taking Stephanie into the tent," Dawn said.

"I want to hear about the monsters," Stephanie protested.

"You're the only monster around here," Dawn told her.

"Well, that's not exactly true," I said. I waited until Dawn carried Stephanie off to the tent, then turned back to Matt, Brian, and Sean. "We'd better stay close to the fire this night," I warned.

"I didn't mention it while we were fishing because from what I've read, the lake is perfectly safe during the day," I continued. "But at night, there have been many unexplained mishaps and strange sightings. Boats have been sunken and fishermen have disappeared mysteriously.

"Legend has it that some large creature has inhabited these waters since ancient times. Late one night, a fisherman accidentally snagged his line on one of the creature's tentacles.

"Imagine the fisherman's surprise when, instead of a bass, a prehistoric sea monster weighing several tons broke the surface of the dark water.

"Not being able to identify the species, and so not knowing whether or not the creature was in season, the fisherman decided to release the beast so as not to invoke the wrath of any local game warden.

"Very quickly, however, the fisherman began to realize that maybe he hadn't caught the monster as much as the monster had caught him. It didn't take a genius to understand that a six-inch-diameter tentacle could easily overcome six-pound-test line and a lightweight rod and reel, no matter how you

137

had set the drag.

"The fisherman wanted to motor away from there as fast as he could, except he was in a row boat. He defended himself the best he could with his fillet knife, but it was no use.

"Having felt the sting of the fisherman's knife, it is said that the creature, to this very day, stalks these waters at night in search of fishermen. And just before dawn, if you look closely through the gray mist, some say you might catch a glimpse of the fisherman in his row boat, lashing out with his fillet knife blindly, because he has no head."

"That's it?" Matt asked. "That wasn't very scary."

"Yeah, it was kind of boring," Brian said. "I think I saw that movie on TV, except it had more blood and more people got killed and it took place in outer space."

"Besides," Sean said. "If the monster lives in the water, we're safe here on land."

"That's what you think," I said. "I haven't told you about the ghost of Jacob Kleigmeier. Kleigmeier was a trapper in these woods more than a hundred years ago.

"One winter, old Jacob was taking a shortcut across the frozen lake. The ice cracked, and Jacob fell through. As he struggled to pull himself out of the water, he could see the light of a campfire on shore. There his partner, Nathan Townes, waited.

"Jacob called out to him for help, but Nathan never came. Jacob froze to death on the ice. Nathan kept his share of the pelts.

"Jacob's ghost still haunts these woods, always preceded by a puff of icy air. He's drawn to the warmth of campfires like ours. He's looking for his pelts, for Nathan, for revenge.

"Thirty years ago, Jacob's ghost appeared and chased a young boy down the logging road five miles, all the way to Quigley's store.

"No one believed the boy's story. He was in therapy for years. He thought his phobia was cured, but when he returned one fall years later to hunt, old Jacob appeared, and again chased him all the way to Quigley's store."

In the glow of the dying campfire I could see the boys yawning, obviously in an attempt to disguise their total fear. I decided to save my really scary bigfoot stories for another night. I ushered the boys into the tent. We climbed into our sleeping bags, and we were soon asleep.

Some time after midnight I was awakened by the chill of an icy puff of air. I jolted upright in my sleeping bag. "Jacob Kleigmeier."

I zipped up the tent window, hoping against the odds that the nylon fabric was more ghost-repellant than the mosquito netting alone. I groped for my flashlight, couldn't find it, but discovered to my horror that the boys were gone.

I went to put on my boots, found one, still wet, then remembered the other had gone up in smoke. I clutched the one wet boot. It was the closest thing I had to a weapon.

I slipped out of the tent as quietly as possible, as if that would make a difference, and there silhouetted in the moonlight was the Grim Reaper himself.

"Back off," I hissed and threw the boot at him. He collapsed on impact. I bent over him and found, under the clothesline, my hooded plastic poncho, the Grim Reaper, my fishing rod his scythe.

The boys were still missing. Then, down by the lake, something slapped the water. It could have been a bass jumping.

"No, be logical," I thought. "It sounded more like a giant tentacle or maybe the oar of a boat piloted by a headless fisherman."

I stumbled, bare-footed, down to the shore. There were the boys, fishing.

"I've got one, Dad," Matt said. His rod arched and his reel whined. I tore the rod from his hands and threw it into the water. Whatever was on the end of the line dragged Matt's rod into the darkness.

There was a noise behind us. We turned and saw a hideous, shadowy image approaching. It could have been Dawn. No, it had to be Jacob!

"Run, boys! Run for your lives! Save yourselves!"

The boys and I raced down the logging road. I felt a little ashamed at my lack of courage, but at least I could tell my therapist I was making progress. At that pace I was sure to cut two minutes off my personal best time to Quigley's store.

Don't Try This
At Home

(Originally published by Game & Fish Publications, October 1994)

Caution: The following contains guidelines for proper etiquette that are recommended solely for use in deer camp and should not be attempted by untrained persons at home.

Most of the guys I know are drawn to deer camp like Pinnochio was drawn to Pleasure Island. In deer camp, guys can temporarily forget everything their mothers ever taught them about civilized living.

There's no one to tell them to keep their elbows off the table or to brush their teeth after every meal. The guys can freely complain about their employers in whatever terminology comes to mind, and of course, there's the opportunity to hunt deer for a few days.

But while the hunters are naively enjoying the camaraderie of reveling in the seeming absence of social restriction, and are busy growing donkey ears and tails, there is another subtle, yet pervasive code of behavior that these hunters unwittingly follow. Scientists now refer to it as deer camp etiquette.

Whether you gather with your hunting companions in a tent, cabin, or posh lodge, there is always the danger of committing a deer camp faux pas that could ostracize you from your fellow hunters.

To prevent this, I have outlined below some of the major tenets of deer camp etiquette.

Safety and Ethics. Strict adherence to firearms safety

practices, hunter ethics and game and fish laws are a must.

Dress Codes. Anything in blaze orange or camouflage will do. Classic red hunter plaid will lend an air of tradition to your ensemble. Wool fabrics are always in style. The wearing of modern waterproof, breathable garments, though socially acceptable, could in some circles label you as a trendsetter, a Beau Brummell, or one who basks in ostentatious displays of image and wealth.

Clothing taboos include neckties, patent leather shoes, pink bunny rabbit slippers, and lace handkerchiefs with little running deer embroidered on them.

Displaying New Stuff. There comes a point early in every deer camp when you must display your new stuff. This is the outdoorsman's version of Show and Tell.

Remember, if a hunter ogles at your new gun or scope, it is important and proper deer camp etiquette to ogle sufficiently when he shows his latest acquisition, even if you end up ogling over the new soles on his 20-year-old boots.

Personal Hygiene. Washing your hands periodically is acceptable. Taking a shower is permitted only in extreme circumstances. Shaving while in deer camp is strictly forbidden as it detracts from the overall image of ruggedness. You'll want to impress your wife when you get home with tall tales of having endured the hardships of the wilderness, while down-playing how much you really enjoyed it. A scruffy beard helps.

Picking you nose while listening to a story around the campfire is acceptable, but you should resist the temptation if you are the storyteller, as you are apt to lose part of your audience.

Questions of deer camp etiquette regarding toilet facilities only arise in those camps utilizing the old two-seater outhouses.

If you make your way to the outhouse and find it is already occupied, it is proper to act as if under the belief that there is only one seat, and wait your turn outside.

If you are the first to arrive and someone comes and sits down next to you, should you make polite conversation or should you pretend he's not there and continue to read your magazine? Social experts disagree.

Housekeeping. Hanging wet socks and long underwear in plain view around camp is acceptable and often necessary. Hanging them from another hunter's gun barrel without permission could lead to a misunderstanding.

It is always important to look busy when camp chores are being performed. For instance, after watching John chop firewood for two hours, it would be polite to say, "Hey, John, let me take a swing at that last log."

Then it would be completely proper for you to clutch your back and say, "Hey, Dave, since John and I just finished chopping all of this firewood, would you mind scraping the grease off of yesterday's breakfast dishes?"

Fine Dining. Most foods that won't slip through the fingers are acceptable to eat without the use of a spoon or fork. The old woodsman practice of using a hunting knife in place of a fork should only be tried by those adept at placing a tourniquet on their own tongues.

If the grease dripping off the bacon looks and smells like the same stuff you used to waterproof your boots, make no mention of it. Never complain about dirt in the stew or hair in the mashed potatoes.

If you were in a fine restaurant, you could complain about the fly in your soup. But you're in deer camp, remember, and probably too hungry to notice all of the dirt, hair and bugs in your food, anyway.

You will make a good impression on your hunting companions if you actually heat water to wash the dishes. If you opt to just wipe off the dirty dishes with your shirttail, no one will mind as long as you didn't borrow the shirt.

Card Games. Card games are a tradition in some deer

camps. If you are not a card player, it won't count against you unless, when looking over your friend's shoulder, you shout, "Hey, you've got Gin," when the game being played is poker.

Sleeping Quarters. Snoring is a fact of life and cannot be regulated by social norms. If your deer camp has upper and lower bunks, it is considered a hostile action to climb down from an upper bunk by finding a foothold in the face or other sensitive areas of the guy below.

Practical Jokes. Practical jokes can liven up any deer camp and are socially acceptable as long as they don't involve property damage. In other words, you should probably not borrow another guy's new hunting cap to use as a target for everyone to sight-in, even if you're sure he's the guy who last year put the rag soaked with buck lure into your truck's heating duct.

Field-Dressing. Each hunter should field dress his own deer. It is the obligation of other hunters at the scene to stand around, watch, and occasionally shake their heads as if the hunter is performing the task incorrectly.

Dragging. It is considered thoughtful to allow other hunters who have not yet tagged their deer the chance to help you drag yours. They will tend to drag your deer more quickly if you repeatedly tell them of the great strategy you used to locate the deer, and what a great shot you made.

An additional benefit to this sharing of the dragging honors is that the others are more apt to support you back in camp when you boast how much your deer weighs.

Getting Your Bearings. Toward the end of a day of hunting, if you cross paths with one of your companions who is headed in the opposite direction, and he says he's headed back to camp, don't tell him you were also headed back to camp. It could embarrass him. Instead, turn and go with him. He'll appreciate it more than going out to search for you later.

144

Thrillseekers
Are Nothing New

(Originally published by Game & Fish Publications, August 2000)

Where did all of these thrill-seekers come from all of a sudden?

Take to the woods or the water these days and you'll see that the skateboard generation has grown up. The former daredevils of the grocery store parking lots are now rock climbing, kayaking, hang gliding, mountain biking, and snowshoeing.

I was taking my shotgun for a walk early last fall when I came upon an example of the new outdoorsman. He was a mountain biker who had bent his ride and bruised his ego when his front wheel had gotten caught between a rock and a hard place at 30 mph on a steep downhill run.

"I was on pace for a personal best, too," he lamented, as he tried to patch both bike and body. "Every weekend I'm either trail-hopping on a bike, running the rapids in a kayak or clinging to the side of a cliff by my fingernails. Nothing tops the outdoor sports for sheer exhilaration."

"If you want to get your heart rate up, you could flush a grouse or just sit and have a trophy buck walk up to you," I said. "You'd break fewer bones and lose less blood that way."

To hear him tell it, you'd think he had invented reckless recreation. Obviously, he had never heard of R. Norman Creedmore, who became a local legend shortly after he moved next door to me about 30 years ago. Many people assumed that the "R" in R. Norman stood for "reckless," because he seemed to be prone to spectacular accidents.

I believe that the "R" in R. Norman stood for "reluctant," because he never would have accomplished any feats of daring if left on his own. Thank goodness R. Norman was a wonderfully gullible lad who could be coaxed into all sorts of stunts.

"R. Norman," I explained, "still holds the cycling record down the gorge trail."

"Norman's Nightmare?" asked the biker.

"Named after him," I said. "He did it when we were just 12 years old. We were on our way to Maynard's Pond to do some fishing. You see, kids back then were taking bicycles on trails long before it became trendy for adults. At the top of the gorge trail, I generously offered to let R. Norman try my bike.

"He made his record run," I continued, "without the benefit of an alloy frame, 21-gears, shock absorbers, or even brakes now that I think about it, which was probably why I talked him into switching bikes in the first place. So you see, we had sheer exhilaration in those days too, but usually it was by accident.

"I felt terrible that R. Norman had to spend so much time in the hospital, but some good did come from it. My old bike had earned a reputation as being the fastest in the neighborhood and I sold it to buy my first fly fishing outfit.

"The time I talked R. Norman into going hunting with me, he reluctantly agreed on the condition that we'd leave the bikes home. Of course we were too young to go hunting by ourselves, but I did manage to find where my mother had hidden my slingshot. We filled our pockets with pebbles for ammunition and set off either to shoot a tiger or to discover and capture the last of the living dinosaurs.

"We were delighted to find a small snake, which in our woods was probably the closest thing to a dinosaur we were likely to find. I coaxed R. Norman into taking off one of his socks to use as a safe way to carry the snake home. You new outdoorsmen wear sport sandals, so you aren't aware of the utility of socks. You always know a boy has had a successful hunt when he comes home carrying, instead of wearing, his socks."

"What's so exhilarating about that?" the biker asked.

"The exhilarating part came the next morning as I urged R. Norman to hurry up and come outside because I'd found the perfect tree to jump out of. He was reluctant until I told him the top of the tree was even with Jennifer Skiddle's bedroom window. He grabbed some not too dirty clothes off the floor of his room and mistakenly put on the sock that still had the snake in it.

"The snake bit him on the big toe and we were both at once grateful that the sock hadn't made it to the laundry room where Mrs. Creedmore was sorting the wash at that moment. R. Norman was grateful too, because he figured getting bitten by a snake was probably less painful than jumping out of a tree.

"We discussed whether or not the snake was poisonous. I told him it never hurts to be cautious and offered to cut out the poison with my pocket knife. R. Norman insisted that the snake was not poisonous and noted that it always hurt when I was being cautious and that he had the x-rays to prove it.

"We decided he should soak the toe and that the best place to do that was down at the pond while we tried to net some frogs. It was too far to walk on a toe that was snake-bitten and bikes were still out of the question for R. Norman.

"So I talked him into sneaking his dad's war surplus rubber raft so we could race down the drainage ditch that fed the pond. Just to be safe, we put on life jackets and football helmets. It was a wild ride because the flood waters hadn't completely subsided. We still hold the record for that run too because they fenced off the ditch shortly afterwards for some reason. R. Norman sells insurance now. Funny he's never tried to sell a policy to me."

I watched the biker limp away, dragging his bicycle. I thought I'd make his walk more exhilarating so I cautioned him about the packs of wild coyotes that go crazy when they smell fresh blood. Then I continued on my way. It was a good day for a hunt, and I had brought extra socks.

Rules Of Thumb
For Sportsmen

(Originally published by Game & Fish Publications, March 2001)

Many hunting and fishing techniques are based on the scientific study of wildlife.

Unfortunately, I was forced to give up my own scientific research years ago after my mother looked into my closet and discovered my collection of bugs, all of which, I explained, had mysteriously migrated there of their own accord.

My mother told me she was very disappointed. So was I, because the bugs had eaten most of my freshwater fish collection, which had stayed relatively well preserved until the pickle juice finally evaporated.

Two years of research went out with the weekly trash. I decided to give up my promising career in biology and to become an entrepreneur. I knew my mother wouldn't be disappointed if I was a success in big business. So I started collecting raccoons in the basement in order to manufacture Davy Crockett caps to sell to my friends – but that's another story.

Even with the aid of science, I have discovered, there are too many variables involved to guarantee that we will shoot a deer or catch a fish. Still, there are general guidelines or rules of thumb that we can follow to increase our odds.

As a rule, for instance, deer will move from their feeding areas to their bedding areas early in the morning.

Now, if it wasn't so difficult to get me to move from my feeding and bedding areas early in the morning, I might be able to take advantage of this situation. As it is, the best I can hope for is to move my feeding and bedding areas with me to the woods, where I can engage in a series of snacking and napping episodes throughout the day.

Since I seem to be all thumbs when it comes to the standard hunting and fishing rules of thumb, I've had to establish a different set of general guidelines based on my own experiences.

My friend Dick stopped over the other morning, saw the pillow and blanket on my living room sofa and said, "So let me see your new gun."

You see, Dick was aware of my rule of thumb that whenever I buy a new gun, I end up sleeping on the sofa for at least a week and fending for myself when it comes to meals. This general rule has been so consistent that I now use it to calculate the price of anything I consider buying.

"Ok, if I buy the gun used, it'll be $350. Now, if I figure in the cost of a new scope, a week on the sofa, several meals at the diner when I get sick of peanut butter sandwiches, then, gee, I don't know if I can afford it right now.

"Of course, if I rake the leaves in the yard or clean out the garage first, I might be able to knock a couple of nights on the sofa off of the price."

Sighting-in a gun once I buy it requires special guidelines as well. With a rifle, generally, a round hitting 2 to 3 inches high at 100 yards will be dead on at 200. My "all-thumbs rule of thumb" for this problem states that if a bullet hits 2 to 3 inches high at 100 yards, then at 200 yards it'll be as wide right as a muffed field goal attempt.

My solution? Switch to the metric system. With the metric system, no one can laugh and say that my shot missed by a mile. And when my friends ask about my new gun, I can honestly tell them that I'm shooting one-kilometer groups

150

with it.

Incidentally, the metric system works well with fishing, too. If I mention that I caught a foot-long bass, my friends will say, "That's nice." But if I brag and say, "That monster must have been over 30 millimeters long," they will really be impressed.

An important all-thumbs rule of thumb for me to remember is that my boots will only keep my feet dry for half as long as I spend waterproofing them the night before. Thus, two hours of hard work rubbing goop into my boots will generally net me one hour of dry feet.

Another all-thumbs rule of thumb states that for every five boxes of shotgun shells I buy, I will generally shoot only one bird.

There are all sorts of standard guidelines for judging the age of a deer by examining its teeth (preferably after you shoot it.) My all-thumbs rule of thumb during a hunt states that if, upon examination, my own teeth appear to have taken on the color and texture of the inner bark of the swamp cedar, but don't smell as good, then I've been in the woods too many days and should probably stop home to make sure my family still lives there.

I no longer try to match my fishing line to my rod and reel. To choose the proper fishing line, my all-thumbs rule of thumb states that (for reasons Dick and I don't care to discuss) I should always select fishing line strong enough to keep two men in a canoe from going over a waterfall.

Another standard fishing guideline, depending on the species you're after, is that you generally use larger lures for larger fish. My all-thumbs rule of thumb states the opposite: Use the smallest lures available for all fish. Here's why:

I currently hold the world record for the most years fishing without catching a decent fish. So now I use the smallest lures I can find, knowing that I'll never catch anything larger than baitfish anyway. My hope is that, as I reel in my catch,

151

a larger fish will be attracted by the struggle and swallow the feeble fish I originally hooked.

This may seem like cheating, but since it hasn't really worked yet anyway, I think I'm okay. I'd have to release any fish I caught anyway, because my ruler is metric, and it wouldn't be worth the complicated math to figure out if the fish was of legal length.

Also, there's an added bonus to those tiny lures: Because they're less expensive, I don't have to spend as many nights on the sofa.

Things Break

(Originally published as Game & Fish Publications, July 1999)

The first thing to consider when equipping yourself for the outdoors is that things break.

I have spent a lifetime breaking things outdoors. Sometimes I've broken things through spectacular blunders, such as the time one Fourth of July campout when I tried to use fireworks to light my charcoal grill.

Sometimes things break during slight accidents, such as when I dropped a custom rifle over a cliff during one of those exotic, guided, max-out-your-credit-card hunts. I salvaged the largest splinters of the rifle stock and we use them to hold wild game hors d'oeuvres together at gun club dinners.

Most things, however, break through no fault of my own. They merely decide it's time to fall apart. Things such as boot laces and fishing line normally break at the absolute worst time.

Things broke as if on schedule during a recent weekend fishing trip with my friend, Larry.

"You sure we're bringing enough?" Larry asked as we loaded the trunk of my car. "We've got a long way to go and you don't even have a spare tire."

"You're forgetting that I'm an expert at breaking things," I said. "If we got a flat, I'd only strip the lug wrench trying to get the rusted lug nuts loose. A spare would be useless if I couldn't get the flat tire off."

When we got to Sulfur Lake, Larry didn't show much confidence in my canoe either.

"You sure those patches will hold?" he asked. "I think we should have brought my boat."

"With that outboard motor?" I said. "The higher the technology, the more that can go wrong, remember that. Here, grab a paddle."

"This paddle's split," Larry said. I asked him to get my tool box out of the car. He returned amazed.

"All you have in here is a hammer, a tube of instant glue, about 5,000 safety pins, and a roll of duct tape," he said.

"That's everything you need to make emergency repairs in the field," I said. "When I break things, it usually involves pieces falling off. The glue is for small pieces, the tape for larger pieces, and the safety pins for things torn to pieces.

"When all else fails I pound on the broken thing with the hammer. Even if it doesn't fix the problem, I get to work out some of that anger.

"When I get home I go through all of my file cabinets full of limited lifetime warranty paperwork. The manufacturers just love me. They send the nicest Christmas cards, too."

"I should have known," Larry said. "after seeing that gun you used last fall with the sling, scope and trigger assembly all held on with duct tape. Did that gun ever shoot?"

"It would have," I said, "but the scope fogged. What a waste of tape -- a roll and a half."

Larry wrapped tape around the canoe paddle while I got my fishing gear ready. The first thing I did was reach up and snap the tip off my new spinning rod.

"Just saving myself some time and heartache," I said.
The day's fishing was very ordinary. The tape did wonders at slowing the leak around one of the patches so that only one of us had to bail full time, allowing the other to do some fishing.

There was one little incident. I caught Larry square in the face with my hand during a backcast while he was reaching forward for the cooler.

The collision smashed his sunglasses, broke his front tooth, and sent him flying overboard. The straps of his life jacket tore when I hauled him back into the canoe. Then we had to paddle after the top of his cooler that was drifting away.

That evening in camp we decided to light my gas lantern so we could see to play cards. I scrounged through my pack and came up with a couple of matches and a handful of new mantles.

"You'd better let me do it," Larry said. He seemed irritable. "Those mantles are delicate. You'll destroy them all before we get one to light. Here, you hold my flashlight."

He handed me the flashlight. It immediately went out.

"I think it's the switch," I said.

"How can it be the switch?" Larry snapped. "It's a new flashlight with new batteries. It must be the bulb."

"With me it's always the switch," I said. "Slide switches, push-button switches, switches that twist. I break them all. Maybe if I pound on it with the hammer..."

"Let's just sit by the fire," Larry suggested.

"It'll have to be a small fire," I said. "There's not much wood. Remember my folding saw broke earlier."

When ancient outdoorsmen discovered fire, they invented a whole new way of breaking things. Meltdown and incineration are two of the best ways to destroy even the best outdoor equipment.

"Is that steam coming off my socks or are they smoldering?" Larry asked. "You think the fire's too hot?"

"Judging by that blob of aluminum that used to be the handle of my frying pan, I'd say it was a possibility," I said. "With socks, I've always found that if you wait until you have to snuff out the flames like on roasted marshmallows, you can be sure they're good and dry."

The zippers on the tent door and mosquito netting both jammed when I tried to open them. I worked them free, got inside, then broke them altogether when I tried to zip them closed. I reached for some safety pins.

156

As I got undressed I popped a button off of my jacket. Another safety pin. I got into my sleeping bag, tugged on the zipper and...four more safety pins.

There's no better alarm clock than safety pins in your sleeping bag. As you toss and turn, you're bound to work one loose and it will jab you just about the time you need to wake up to start fishing.

When we were packed for the trip home, it was inevitable that the car wouldn't start.

"It's usually just a loose or rusted wire," I said. I took the hammer and banged away on the battery terminals, the coil, the starter, and several funny looking things.

"Sounds like you're trying to play the drum solo to 'Wipeout,'" Larry said.

"I'm too young to remember that," I said. "Turn the key again." This time the engine started like an old race car, meaning that we had to push it a ways to jump-start it.

When I got home, I told my wife, Dawn, about the weekend.

"I fixed his sunglasses with tape, used safety pins to repair his torn life jacket and even put a strip of tape on his cooler so the lid wouldn't float away again," I said. "He wouldn't let me hammer on his flashlight. I think he was mad."

"Why would he be mad?" Dawn asked.

"The glue," I said. "It bonds too quickly. If he would've stood still, I don't think the tooth would have ended up so crooked."

Ponderings
Of A Stump-Sitter

(Originally published by Game & Fish Publications, November 2001)

Most deer hunters, I've discovered, are people, too. So it's not surprising that, despite our common interests, you will find a wide variety of peculiar personality traits within our slightly obsessed, slightly maniacal little segment of society.

With other types of hunters, you know what to expect. Duck hunters, for instance, are willing to sit all day long in cold, wet places because they enjoy each other's company as much as they enjoy shooting ducks.

Upland bird hunters are a more introspective sort. They would just as soon keep company with a good hunting dog as with another hunter. They roam the fields and woods reminiscing about old shotguns and pondering philosophical issues such as whether or not they really prefer side-by-sides to over-and-unders, or pump guns to semi-autos.

But deer hunters don't fit quite so neatly into a standard mold.

One season, while I waited patiently for the grandpappy of all bucks to happen by, I found that I had exhausted ways to make efficient use of my downtime in the deer stand.

I had already taken a short nap, counted the eyelets on my boots twice (starting from different directions to make sure I arrived at the same number both times), eaten my lunch, rested my eyes again for a few minutes, and discovered that if I connected the dings on my gun stock, I could form 17 constellations: the Big Dipper, the Little Dipper, and 15 I invented myself.

Not being one who likes to squander precious time, I decided to begin categorizing deer hunting's dominant personality types.

Using subjective reflection, with no reliance on logic or any other scientific basis, I was able to sort my own small group of hunting acquaintances into the following distinct types:

The Competitor. This breed of deer hunter is always trying to outperform you. If you arrive back at camp exhausted and exclaim that you must have walked 10 miles, the Competitor will bounce up and insist that he easily walked 15. If you shoot a buck, he'll congratulate you — and then mention that he passed up a shot that day at a much larger deer.

The Stump-Sitter. This hunter doesn't put any pressure on himself. Nor does he care that he's got the most beat-up gun in the group. He's content to let the world pass by as he sits back and enjoys the view. Unfortunately for the Competitors, it is often the Stump-Sitters who, without really trying and without really caring, end up shooting the best deer.

The Daredevil. "Go for it! Your truck's got plenty of ground clearance." For this guy, the hard way is the only way. He's the one who suggests it would be much quicker to rappel straight down the gorge using the emergency fishing line in his pack. Fording a stream, navigating through a swamp or blazing a shortcut through a thorny thicket, the Daredevil never has a mishap — it's always the guy stupid enough to follow him who gets into trouble.

The Wanderer. Never plan a rendezvous with a Wanderer. He's too easily distracted to meet you at any specific time and place. He's a compulsive explorer, always curious to see what's over the next ridge or around the next bend. He often forgets that he's supposed to be hunting.

The Strategist. This guy over-analyzes every situation. He'll study maps, weather, terrain and deer sign to form a hypothesis on where the deer are hiding. If he's wrong, he's not discouraged: he just starts over with a new theory. Never let a Strategist plan a deer drive! He'll make things more complicated than a military maneuver.

The Party Pooper. "Go on ahead without me, guys — I'll be all right": That's the war cry of the Party Pooper. This guy is gung-ho during the planning stages of a hunt, but as soon as there is any effort or hardship involved, the Party Pooper begins his feel-sorry-for-me whining.

The Impostor. The impostor talks a good game, but rarely hunts. He'll tell and retell the same tall hunting tales, embellishing them over the years with bits and pieces of other hunters' experiences. If you actually invite him on a hunt, he'll find an excuse to explain why he can't go.

The Housekeeper. This type of hunting partner is constantly preoccupied with setting up and maintaining a pristine camp complete with elaborately planned meals. He'll keep trying to sweep the floor if you don't remind him periodically that it's dirt.

The Perfect Partner. Combine the best traits of each type and you'd have the Perfect Hunting Partner.

This guy would compete with you just enough to keep you on your toes, but wouldn't mind losing. He'd know when to just sit and relax, but if he had a bit of the Wanderer in him, he'd understand it if you didn't make the rendezvous because you did a little exploring of your own.

It's good to have a plan sometimes, so being part Strategist wouldn't be bad, and the boldness of the Daredevil could be a plus when the going gets tough. I'd rather have a Housekeeper in camp than a slob, and a Party Pooper at least knows when it's time to go home.

Force an Impostor to go hunting with you once — no excuses accepted — and he'll boast about your hunting exploits together for years, thus transforming you into a local legend.

Of course, you may never find the Perfect Hunting Partner. But if you don't, you can always do what I do. I team the Competitor with the Daredevil and hope they both survive. I let the Strategist pace back and forth to wait for the Wanderer. I leave the Party Pooper in camp to help the Housekeeper, and I never have to worry about the Impostor, because he always finds a reason not to come.

Where does that leave me? Sitting on a stump somewhere resting my eyes and waiting for the grandpappy of all bucks to happen by.

The Perfect R.V.

(Originally published by Game & Fish Publications, August 2001)

If getting there is half the battle, then for most of my life I've been losing the war.

You'd think that an outdoorsman would live in a place where it was convenient to pursue his passions. I've often envisioned what it would be like to live in a cabin on the side of a gentle slope. There, I could walk out on my front porch in the morning to see trout jumping in a picturesque stream that would flow into a deep blue lake. I'd watch as the sun rose over the endless forested hills beyond.

I've envisioned strolling around to the back yard, where I could watch with amusement as my dog chased rabbits and flushed birds among the wildflowers. Far off, where the meadow would fade into a stand of hardwoods, I would spy movement. Raising my binoculars, I'd spot a flock of turkeys intermingled with dozens of large-racked whitetails.

By the way, if you live in such a place, prepare yourself for a shock: I am your long-lost son. Please send me your address so that I can return home).

The sad truth of the matter, however, is that once you find such a paradise, other people will begin to accumulate there like mold on last month's I-don't-know-what-it-used-to-be food in the back of the refrigerator.

People tend to clutter once-perfect places with schools, gas stations, grocery stores, bowling alleys, apartment complexes and lots of convenient parking for old folks who say, "I

162

remember when none of this stuff used to be here."

I grew up in the clutter of a residential neighborhood. So once I found myself afflicted with the hunting and fishing bug, I immediately became a carrier — not of any disease, mind you, but of the equipment essential to my pursuit of game and fish.

Unlike my dream home, my real home was rather limited in terms of nearby sporting possibilities. As soon as the squirrel that lived in a tree in my back yard noticed that I was old enough to sharpen sticks and throw stones, it decided to take up residence elsewhere. That pretty much exhausted all my close-to-home hunting and fishing options. Thus began my lifelong career as an equipment carrier, traveling endlessly from one hunting or fishing destination to another.

Since I wasn't allowed to cross the street by myself, I had to cut through neighbors' backyards to reach prospective new areas. I usually made it about as far as Mrs. Feldman's yard, three houses away, when I'd get tired and decide this was as good of a place as any to set up camp.

I rigged an old piece of clothesline from the back of Mrs. Feldman's garage to her bird feeder and then draped the quilt from my sister's bed over the top to form a tent. But when my mother called me for dinner, I left everything where it was and ran home. Three days later, when the rain finally stopped, I retrieved the equipment and, being a good brother, returned the quilt to my sister's bed.

When I was a little older, my bicycle became my first recreational vehicle. This greatly increased my range, which was good, because the hunting around Mrs. Feldman's bird feeder became a lot more difficult after she learned to keep an eye out for me.

My first bicycle was a hand-me-down with balloon tires that had been repaired so many times that the inner tubes looked like strings of linked sausages. But the amount of equipment I could carry was still pretty limited, even when I tied my red wagon to the back as a trailer.

My parents had hoped a college education would transform me into a normal, responsible person. But during those years, I had also acquired an old Buick. With its enormous trunk, spacious back seat and overflow capacity on the roof (to say nothing of what I could hang out of the windows), I could carry all the gear I needed. The Buick made a wonderful recreational vehicle.

"Who needs four-wheel-drive?" I'd say to my friends. "All we need to do is get a good running start and keep up the momentum. Hold on!"

With fuel at 30 cents a gallon, that Buick took us on many faraway adventures. Unfortunately, it didn't always bring us back.

"This looks like as good a place as any to set up camp," I'd say. "It may be days before they can get us out, anyway. Let's draw straws to see who walks out for help once the rain stops. And remember — winches alone won't do it. They'll need chain saws, too."

For years after I retired the Buick, I backpacked to most of my hunting and fishing destinations. I didn't see the need for another recreational vehicle. But about the time I turned 40, I noticed I wasn't having as much fun sitting on a stump in the rain, huddled under a poncho I'd rigged into a lean-to with an old piece of clothesline, with a mini-flashlight dangling from my mouth as I tried to light my one-burner stove.

Sleeping on the ground and then trying to resume my role as equipment carrier the next day was torture. Forty-year-old backs and 50-pound packs are not compatible.

So rather than lighten the load, I decided to unite everything I owned in one special-purpose mobile base camp — a true recreational vehicle with a kitchen, a four-burner stove and refrigerator, a bathroom, a heater that works, and sleeping accommodations for six.

Now I could enjoy the outdoors from inside my RV, because

it had lots of big windows. Finally, I could take all of my stuff anywhere.

So even though it was raining hard as I backed my new rig into the camp site, I wasn't concerned. I was searching for the button to turn on the rear wiper when I heard a crunching sound, similar to what you might hear if an RV backed over a picnic table.

"This," I declared, pulling on the parking brake, "looks like as good of a place as any."

The Farm Pond
Follies

(Originally published by Game & Fish Publications, June 1994)

It's 7 a.m. Saturday morning and even the sun seems to be taking its time to rise. There's is a cloud of mist over the old farm pond, nearly obscuring the children's playground and an open-sided pavilion beyond in the place where corn used to grow.

An insect seems to chase its reflection as it hovers close to the surface of the pond. Suddenly a trout leaps out of its hiding place, grabs the insect and slaps back into the water.

In my bedroom it's also 7 a.m. Saturday morning, meaning I too am in no hurry to start the day. I have not yet broken the surface to consciousness when suddenly my youngest son, Sean, leaps through the air and splashes down to the surface of my water bed accurately jabbing one bony foot squarely into my abdomen.

He is followed by Brian, half again bigger and Matt, twice as big. With one son prying my eyelids with his fingertips, another using my belly as a trampoline and the third tickling the bottoms of my feet, I bid adieu to Dreamland.

My wife, Dawn, responds to my moans for help by saying, "Don't be such a grouch. It's time to get up."

8 a.m. Cars begin to pull into the dirt parking lot next to the old farm pond, past the hand-painted sign that reads, "Kids' Fishing Derby Saturday 9 AM to Noon."

I am in one of those cars, pondering the notion that the

166

average trout stocked in the pond has, with whatever insects it has consumed, eaten more for breakfast than I have.

"Hurry up Dad," the boys say. "All the good spots will be taken."

The boys bolt out of the car. Dawn raises her camera and takes a photo of me trying to juggle the rods, tackle boxes, and lawn chairs for the march to the pond.

As we set up the lawn chairs to establish squatters' rights, I notice a man and a little girl standing next to me. They have no chairs, no stools, no buckets to sit on. They have no ponchos, no umbrellas, no tackle boxes, no video cameras. All they have is a fishing rod and a can of worms.

"Your first fishing derby?" I ask the man.

"Yes. How did you know?"

"You have no large, stumble-over items to mark your boundaries. See how we've strategically spaced our lawn chairs? When the kids start casting, you'll want plenty of elbow room. That way you'll have fewer flying objects to dodge.

"Also, if you have to take your kid to the bathroom, you won't lose your place along the shore. The winner in the eight-year-old division last year caught his fish in this exact spot. Of course we weren't in this spot last year. We were down that way a little further. Got here late. Didn't catch a thing. That's why we got here early this year.

"You need ponchos or umbrellas too because no matter what day they choose for the derby, it usually rains. If you're prepared for it you can stay for the whole derby while most of the others leave.

"Since they award prizes for first, second and third in every age category, you're almost assured of being a winner if you catch any old fish at all.

"The prizes are almost always new rod and reel combos, which works out well because if you plan on coming to the derby every year, you'll need a new rod and reel every year to

167

replace the one your child breaks at the derby every year."

"Well," the man says, "we're just here for the fun of it."

"Ha!" I laughed. "I felt the same way our first derby. Wait until it seems that everyone around you is catching fish except your kid. That puts more pressure on you than trying to win the big purple unicorn at the state fair.

"Naturally you don't want your child to feel left out or to go home disappointed. So you re-rig and try harder. The parents next to you see you trying harder, so they try harder.

"You've started a chain reaction that intensifies with each revolution around the pond until it's parent versus parent, all in the name of fun for the kids, who by this time are more interested in the free hotdogs and ice cream."

The man takes his daughter's hand and ushers her off to the opposite side of the pond.

"Nice meeting you," I call after him, but he just keeps walking.

8:30 a.m. The boys come back covered up to their knees and up to their elbows in mud.

"We caught a frog." they proclaim.

"No, I caught it," Matt says.

"No, I caught it," Sean says.

"You caught it, but it got away," Matt says. "So then I caught it."

"But I caught it first," Sean insists.

"I'm the one who spotted it," Brian says. "So it's really mine."

"It doesn't matter," I say. "We're not keeping it."

Dawn takes a photo of the muddy boys and their frog.

9 a.m. An army of youngsters brandishing fishing rods is a sight that could scare away invading Mongol hordes. An official uses a bullhorn to signal the start of the derby and instantly there is a hailstorm of bobbers pelting the pond's surface.

9:05 a.m. The first fish is caught and placed in a large

168

plastic bucket. All of the young contestants gather around to admire the catch and to stick their arms in the bucket.

Word spreads quickly among the parents: He used two split shot in line, a single hook baited with a worm at a depth of six feet. Bobbers are adjusted and, with a tremendous whine of a hundred reels, there is another mass flight of hooks, line and sinkers.

The only documented safe place to stand is next to the target set up for the ongoing casting accuracy contest behind the pavilion.

9:30 a.m. The ranks of the contestants suffer their first losses as those with the shortest attention spans migrate to the playground equipment.

10:30 a.m. The official with the bullhorn reappears to announce that the hotdogs are ready. There is a mass exodus to the pavilion. Parents, abandoned, are now the only ones still fishing.

As the last of my sons sprints away, my request to have him bring back a hotdog for "old Dad" goes unheard. I am anchored to the shoreline holding three fishing rods whose lines, together with those of our neighboring contestants on both sides, have somehow braided themselves into a single length of rope.

11 a.m. A trout tugs at the line. I look over my shoulder, but none of my sons is in view. Knowing there's no time to be lost, I reach down and latch onto the collar of a passing contestant.

"I have a fish on. Reel him in quickly."

I hand him the rods, he hands me his half-eaten hotdog in a mangled bun with a perfect set of his dirty fingerprints on it. He lands the fish by running away from the pond holding up the tangled lines as if he was flying a kite.

"Thanks, mister." The boy runs off with his fish. Dawn reappears to take a photo of me with mustard trickling down my shirt as I stuff the remainder of the kid's hotdog in my mouth.

11:30 a.m. The official with the bullhorn announces that all contestants who have caught fish should now go to the pavilion for the official measuring and recording. It starts to rain.

Noon. The awards ceremony begins under the pavilion. Dawn takes a photo of the strange boy holding up my fish in one hand and the new fishing rod and reel combo he's won in the other. I slink away, hoping he won't see me and ask for his hotdog back.

12:15 p.m. The rain stops. We pack up the tangle of rods and line, lawn chairs and tackle boxes and trudge through the mud back to the car. I glance back to see Sean toss a crumb of his hotdog bun into the water. A trout rises and slurps it in.

12:30 p.m. Everyone's aboard and we wait in line to get out of the parking lot. A frog hops out from under my driver's seat and sits looking at me from between the gas and brake pedals.

The boys say they wish there was a fishing derby every Saturday.

An Outdoorsman's Valentine

Originally published by Game & Fish Publications, February 2002)

Valentine's Day: I should have known. It falls smack-dab between the time I stow my hunting gear and when I re-organize my tackle box. But I'd forgotten all about it until my 6-year-old daughter, Stephanie, handed me a heart-shaped card she'd made out of red construction paper. The poem scrawled in crayon started with large letters that gradually tapered down, curving sideways as they reached the far edge of the paper.

Oh, Daddy, be my Valentine —
You are the best with gun and line.

To me you're super, even though
You often miss or let them go.
I want to be like you someday;
If I keep trying, I just may.
You took me fishing once, it's true:
I caught a bigger bass than you.
Don't feel bad; I've beaten others.
(I am a girl with three big brothers.)

I now know how to whittle sticks
(That's not too bad — I just turned six).
I've earned my own fleece camo suit;
It's nearly time I learned to shoot.
And in another year or two,
When I go on a hunt with you,
I promise that I won't make noise;
I will hunt better than the boys.

Love, Stephanie

"Did you write that all by yourself?" I asked.
"Mom helped me," she admitted.
"I thought so."
One thing was certain: My wife, Dawn, wouldn't forget. There was no time even to order flowers. Desperate, I took my lead from Stephanie.
"Get the construction paper and crayons for me, please," I said. "I'm going to make a card for Mommy."

172

With my daughter's help, I soon crafted a card and a poem that I thought just might save my neck.

Valentine For My Wife

To you a tribute, my dear wife
Who never bargained for this life.
To be so stressed, so taxed, so harried,
These twenty years since we were married.

It all began so long ago,
When Cupid shot his compound bow.
Though most accounts depict him bare
While launching arrows in the air,
This time he came all dressed in camo,
On neither of us spared his ammo.
The little hunter from above
Twice hit his mark; we called it love.

Your mom, upset; the news did rock her
When it was clear you'd wed no doctor.
I was not one for that profession;
To hunt and fish was my obsession.

You must have seen what lay in store —
Such telltale signs you can't ignore.
A skeet range: the prophetic setting
Of what became our shotgun wedding.

Our honeymoon? No posh resort,
Nor ocean cruise of any sort.
The romance that you might have wished
Lay not in camping while I fished.

For you, instead of kisses, hugs,
Were toting wood and swatting bugs.
You could have gotten out of there
With ever-ready taxi fare,
But you pretended it was fun,
Although dark clouds replaced the sun.
(It was the best time ever spent,
While huddled in a leaky tent.)

And through the years as I look back,
I've often left with gun and pack,
Left job and chores for no good reason,
Except that it was — yes! — deer season.

You've put up with my muddy boots,
My turkey calls and hoot-owl hoots,
My grubby clothes and scruffy beard,
My hunting pals you think are weird.

The dog I bought for chasing rabbits
Developed ever more bad habits.
He tore the drapes and chewed your shoes
When paper-trained, was front-page news.

And all the time I roamed about
In search of bigger bass and trout,
You never doubted or poked fun
At endless tries to catch just one.

I've had so many guns and knives
(Amazing — not as many wives).
I bought whatever caught my eye;
Our plans to budget went awry.

In anger you would rarely shout,
Despite the things you did without.
You must have looked down on your luck
The years you drove our rusty truck.
You scrimped and saved, and, heaven knows,
You could have used some more new clothes.

And then with children we were blessed;
We had three boys (you might have guessed).
At times we men gang up on you,
For they're all into fishing, too.
Then came a daughter you could pamper;
To your dismay, she's now a camper.
Who would have thought that one so small
Would love the outdoors most of all?
You are tops, the best, a winner —
So sit back now while I make dinner;
Just promise you'll sit next to me.
I'll whip up some old recipe.
No leftovers, no burgers, fries —
Tonight, my special: Squirrel Surprise.

I'm sorry for the pain and strife —
So be my Valentine, dear wife.
No candy box, no rose bouquet:
You might think I forgot this day.
A special gift I had all planned —
I nearly had it in my hand.
This fishing rod — so shiny-new,
Could I resist? — perhaps will do.
(I really bought it, Love, for you.)

A Bad Day
For Fishing

(Originally published by Game & Fish Publications, April 1999)

If you're hiking along and happen to notice that the trail ends abruptly with a 300-foot drop into a gorge, you can probably figure without a calculator that, unless you are wearing a parachute, taking one more step might ruin your day.

Sadly, not all harbingers of ill fortune are so obvious to outdoorsmen. We continue on, blind to the telltale signs that point to trouble on the path ahead.

Take your average day of fishing, for instance. You awaken at 5 a.m., not to the sound of your alarm clock, but to the rumbling of thunder and the flash of lightning in your window.

This should clue you in that it might be a bad day for fishing. So you roll over, put your pillow over your head and try to get back to sleep, right?

No, of course not. You decide the storm's just passing through. You're late. You stumble out of bed, take a look in the mirror at the tufts of your hair sticking out in all directions and say to yourself, "Naw, I don't need a shower. I'll just put on my fishing cap."

You go to the kitchen table, and by the light of the open refrigerator door, you hastily throw together one of your on-the-run breakfasts: in this case last night's leftover Chinese takeout.

You should suspect that the day is getting off to a bad start when you notice the vegetables in the bowl seem to be squirming when you poke them with your fork.

Instead you count yourself fortunate that you've realized before your first bite that you must have grabbed the bait containers out of the refrigerator by mistake.

You ignore another obvious warning sign. If the bait doesn't wiggle more than that on your fork, it certainly won't be any more lively on the hook.

Still, you grab the remaining bait containers from the refrigerator and head out, thinking you might still have the appetite for the donuts you can pick up on the way.

You're an hour late meeting your friend, Tom, at the marina. He takes this as a good omen, since you are normally an hour and a half late.

"You remember Tom Junior," he says. "He's coming along with us today."

You look at Tom Junior, a lad of about 12, sporting the same bowling pin profile as Tom Senior, and you remember him well enough to know you should make an excuse, turn around, and head home immediately. Instead, you offer Junior a donut. He takes three.

The thunder and lightning subsides to what looks like an all-day drizzle as you wait in line at the launch ramp. This is a good sign, you figure. With all of these guys here, waiting to get on the lake, the fishing must be good.

You finally get your turn on the ramp and help Tom get his boat in the water, only to find that Tom can't get the outboard motor started.

You could take this as an indication that it will be a bad day for fishing. Instead, you find you're still in luck, as Junior reminds his dad that the battery on the electric trolling motor has nearly a full charge.

Tom mans the trolling motor while Junior takes a seat next to you. You try to start a conversation, but find it difficult to maintain eye contact with someone who has one finger up his nose most of the time. "Like father, like son," you say to yourself, a sure sign that you're in for a long day.

You start to rig your line and Tom says, "Pay close attention to how he does things, Junior. You may learn something."

Talk about putting a jinx on somebody. You know it's going to be a bad day for fishing when you're expected to actually catch a fish to show a youngster how it's done.

It would be much better to get him involved, you think. Hands-on experience, that's the ticket. So you hand Junior the bait container to get him started.

"No thanks," he says. "I don't like Chinese food."

You look into the container and to your amazement, not only did you bring along the Chinese takeout instead of the bait you almost had for breakfast, but you actually found a food substance that Junior won't eat.

Without missing a beat, you announce with confidence that you'll be fishing with artificials. You open your tackle box and look over the fine selection of bass plugs, mostly unused since you always fish with live bait.

You know it's going to be a bad day for fishing, since you're fishing for trout, not bass.

So you rig your line again and make your best cast, keeping in mind that Junior is carefully scrutinizing your every move. Except Junior isn't paying attention to you at all. Junior is busy reeling in a 20-inch trout that bit on a piece of your leftover sweet-and-sour chicken.

You know it's going to be a bad day for fishing when the novice in the group immediately catches a large fish. It practically guarantees that you won't catch anything larger than stunted sunfish even if they do have a taste for Chinese food.

Luckily, flashes of lightning begin to appear again on the horizon and you mention to Tom that he might want to start heading to shore.

If you really need to get somewhere in a hurry, it's easy to predict that something will prevent you from doing it.

So, naturally, the battery to the trolling motor dies, prompting Tom and you to rekindle the age-old debate on whether to use the one oar to paddle the boat like a canoe or to pole it like a Venetian gondola.

The discussion is beneficial if for no other reason than to prevent Junior from using his one-fish expertise to lecture you on how to catch large trout.

Once ashore Junior does his share to help tote the gear back to the cars.

"Here, let me take that," you say to him, taking back your expensive fishing rod before he does something disastrous to it. Then you turn and promptly slam the car door on it, smashing the tip section to shreds.

After this kind of day, you're thankful to get home, where your wife is surprised to see you since you're only an hour late for dinner, instead of the usual hour and a half.

"What's for dinner," you ask.

"The leftover Chinese food," she replies.

The next time you come to that 300-foot gorge, you tell yourself, you might just as well step off.

It's Never Too Late

(Originally published by Game & Fish Publications, December 2002)

My mother told me that I arrived in this world a little earlier than expected. I've been late for everything since.

I was late for my first day of school and my last day of final exams. Two alarm clocks and my wife Dawn's cold feet nudging me out of bed can't keep me from being habitually late for work. And it's no coincidence that the editor puts my column on the last page of this magazine every month. Most of all, when I've been out hunting, fishing, or just roaming around outdoors, I'm late getting home.

"I know, I know. I was supposed to be home hours ago," I told Dawn one evening. "I'll probably be late for my own funeral, too."

"No," she said. "I'm sure when it comes to your funeral, you just won't show up at all. You'll go off hunting some day and just never come back. We'll have a nice service without you, though. With you not there, at least I know it will start on time."

Dawn says that I'm a procrastinator, too, and one of these days I'll get around to asking her just what she means by that. Being late isn't the same thing, however. A procrastinator continually puts things off to a later time. A "S.N.A.I.L.", Someone Nearly Always Inexcusably Late, has every intention of being on time, but is easily side-tracked and can't seem to shift beyond first gear.

Here's an example: My friend Sid asked me to go bird hunting with him. He wanted me to meet him at his house at

180

6:00 the next morning, but knowing I'd be late, he told me to be there at 5:30.

I wanted to be there on time, so I got all my gear together the night before. All I had to do in the morning was to pull on my brush pants and my boots and head out the door. Figuring it was just a 10-minute ride to Sid's house, I set my alarm clock for 5 a.m.

When the alarm went off, I reached out and slapped at it blindly to stop it from shrieking. I lay there for fifteen minutes, struggling to make the transition from sleep to consciousness, knowing I had time because Dawn always sets the clock ahead 10 minutes for my benefit.

Once up, I figured I still had 15 minutes to spare -- plenty of time for a quick breakfast. I poured myself a bowl of cereal, took one spoonful and decided that the labeling on the box didn't offer the proper reading material to aid my digestion. Reading material, as you probably know, is important in every phase of digestion, and should be readily available in both the kitchen and the bathroom.

I went to the front door to get the morning paper. The paper reported the usual political debate over how best to spend my tax dollars on government programs to combat social upheaval domestically and to perpetrate it abroad. Or was it the other way around? The weather report was useful, however, and it predicted colder than normal weather.

I wondered if I should give those socks with the integral battery-operated heaters one more try. What kind of batteries did they need? I pawed through the household junk drawer where the odds and ends of a hundred undone repair projects were optimistically stored by an ambitious wife for her procrastinator husband.

I found batteries, but were they any good? I decided to test them in my daughter Stephanie's portable radio. Where would a six-year-old hide a radio? I tiptoed into her room, checked her closet, her dresser, and under her bed. There it was in a corner, forming part of a wall for the exclusive seaside resort she had built for her glamour girl dolls.

Back in the kitchen I installed the batteries and turned on the radio. It worked. Then, still a little drowsy, I paused for a moment to try to remember why I had wanted the radio. Then came the updated news and weather report: "And at 5:30, it's 29 degrees."

It was the time, not the temperature that sent chills down my spine. I was late again. No problem. I'd forget about breakfast, simply get dressed, be out the door in five minutes and arrive at Sid's at 5:45. I was sure he'd wait a mere 15 minutes for me.

I ran into a slight stumbling block when I found the windshield of my truck iced over. The defroster would take too long. I scraped out a peek hole in the windshield with the cereal spoon I still had in my hand for some reason.

I was on my way. Then, about three blocks from my house, I saw the emergency lights behind me.

"You didn't make a complete stop at that intersection back there," the officer said.

He might have let me go, but I had forgotten my wallet. No wallet, no license, no problem. All I had to do was to sit and wait for him to check me through the computer and then to write the ticket. I turned on the wipers, put the defroster on high and tried to clear the rest of the windshield. I looked at the clock on the dashboard. "7:00."

"Thank goodness that clock's been displaying the wrong time for two years," I thought. "I should learn how to reset it. The gas gauge isn't right, either, but that probably just needs a new fuse. I'll get it fixed one of these days."

After the policeman pulled away, I put my truck in gear and it stalled. When several attempts to restart it failed, I decided to save what was left of the battery.

"See, I was right," I thought. "The gas gauge is broken."

I grabbed the empty gas can from the back of the truck and

182

started for the nearest all-night convenience store.

I pumped the gas, then remembered I didn't have my wallet. No wallet, no money, no problem. I left the gas can, ran back to the truck, scrounged through the glove box, in the ash tray, and under the seats until I found a couple of dollars in change. Then it was back to the gas station, then back to the truck with the gas, then a quick stop back home for my wallet.

I pulled in to Sid's driveway at 6:20.

"Sid will be right with you," his wife told me. "He woke up a little bit late."

"No problem," I said. "It's happened to me before."

Retrieving
Outdoor Memories

(Originally published by Game & Fish Publications, March 2003)

Human memory is like a lousy shot pattern. It's hit and miss. And as it gets further along, it covers a larger area, but leaves larger gaps, hitting on bits of things almost at random despite your specific aim, until it's entirely inaccurate.

As I get older, I don't want to have to depend solely on my memory when it comes to recalling the great times I've had outdoors. So over the years I've accumulated drawers and boxes full of photos, journals, and artifacts to help jog my memory whenever I want to reminisce.

Preserving outdoor memories through photography has several drawbacks:

If you shoot the photos yourself, you'll never be in them. You'll never develop half the rolls of film you shoot. Who needs double prints of people with their feet and heads cut out of the frames? In scenic photos the sun's always too bright and the shadows too dark.

And unless you label them, you will eventually forget when you took them and why, thus negating the reason for taking photos in the first place.

Eyewitness accounts can sometimes document a notable deed better than any old photo or souvenir. An eyewitness not only helps you to recall what happened, but can lend credibility to your story.

To ensure an eyewitness recalls a story the same way you

do, it's advisable to make him part of the action.

"That was a huge bass that Barlow caught - five pounds at least," said Dave, an excellent eyewitness whom I'd been training for years. That reference to a huge, five-pound bass helped to jog my memory. Now, in turn, I had to reward Dave by making him integral to the story.

"Well, that's true, Dave," I said. "It probably was the biggest fish ever caught on that lake. But I never could have landed it if you hadn't been so skillful with the net."

Notice how humble I was. Next, a proper eyewitness should add more suspense or perhaps a touch of humor.

"I was so excited because your fish was so big," Dave chuckled, "that I fumbled the net and fell overboard trying to get control of it."

"Yet even in the water, you bravely held onto the net," I recalled.

"Yeah, then you wouldn't let me back in the boat until I first handed you the net with your stupid fish in it." Dave's training as an eyewitness was not yet complete at the time.

Each time a story is retold, a little of what really happened gets lost in the translation. Gaps in memory are filled in with embellishments to make the tale more dramatic or to make the teller more heroic or less liable.

Because of this, wives usually do not make very good eyewitnesses. They have little understanding of how to accurately recall such important events. Take the same story with my wife Dawn as the eyewitness.

"Remember that big bass I caught?" I asked.

"I remember one breaking your line," Dawn replied. "You had one of your typical temper tantrums and blamed me for not getting the net quickly enough. Come to find out, you'd forgotten to bring the net anyway."

See how they twist the truth? Don't have your wife as your eyewitness.

185

If a story is notable enough, eventually someone writes it down and it becomes history. When that historical account is no longer in fashion, it is rewritten to suit the political tastes of the day.

I have long kept journals of my outdoor activities. Someday they will serve as my personal history to be shared and treasured by my descendants.

"Why are you tearing all of those pages out of your journals," Dawn asked.

"It wouldn't be honest to rewrite history just to make myself look better," I said. "So I decided to edit out that story about the five-pound bass. Besides, it wasn't written the way I remember it now, ten years later. I'm saving only those journal entries on the things that might someday be considered historic."

"I don't know that you've ever done anything historic," Dawn said. "But I can attest that your behavior is continually pre-historic."

Sometimes your most treasured memories are contained in the little artifacts you bring home with you. When my children were quite young, their artifacts were simple. They'd pick a dandelion for Dawn and hand little stones to me.

Little stones are universal in their appeal as memory artifacts. When a scientist discovers a lost civilization, what does he bring back with him? Little stones.

And remember when Neil Armstrong wanted us to believe he walked on the moon? From his little outdoor adventure he brought back some scratchy video that looked like it was shot by the same guy who did the Bigfoot film and, no surprise, a box of little stones.

Animals or pieces of animals are also popular outdoor memory artifacts. Going camping with the kids? Bring containers for worms, bugs, snakes, turtles, lizards, and leave lots of room for stray dogs and cats.

For three months, we had a stray dog we fondly called

186

Rabies, until he wandered off and became someone else's artifact. My memory fails me on how we came by him, but each of the kids has his own story, backed by eye witness testimony.

If they can't bring back the whole animal, sometimes kids will be content with just a piece - a bird feather or perhaps some unidentified bone. This actually shows some maturity, for as adult hunters and fishermen, the animals we bring home, for convenience sake, are mostly dead and in pieces, packaged to be cooked and eaten at a later date.

On one dark occasion, however, our daughter Stephanie opened the door to the freezer in the basement, looking for ice cream, and shrieked when she was confronted there by a completely intact, but somewhat frosty red fox.

"How did that thing get in there?" Dawn demanded.

Thank goodness there were no eyewitnesses to jog my memory.

"I don't remember," I said.

Calling In A Specialist

(Originally published by Game & Fish Publications, January 2005)

"People used to be self-reliant," I told my wife, Dawn. "Hand me that wrench will you? They had to do things for themselves. They couldn't just pick up the telephone every time they needed something done."

"Mike at the garage said it sounded like your truck might need a new computer chip," she said. "He's got the specialized diagnostic equipment to test that."

"Nonsense," I said. "It's just running a little rough. It's probably a loose spark plug. I don't understand why they build these things so you have to dismantle half the engine to get to something that looks vaguely familiar."

"I don't understand why you have to fiddle with it when we're five miles from the nearest paved road," she said. "I think you're upset because you didn't catch any fish, and now you're taking your frustrations out on the truck."

"I'm just going to tweak it a little before we go."

"With all of today's advanced technology, it takes years to become proficient in any one discipline," Dawn said. "It's difficult to be a jack-of-all-trades. We have to specialize and auto mechanics will never be your specialty."

"That's the trouble," I said. "Hand that screwdriver to me. We live in a world of specialization. We are trained to know and do one thing. For anything else, we depend on a network of specialists who have the expertise we don't. Ouch! There's still some life in that battery. I hate being dependent

on anyone for anything."

"If you're sick, you depend on a doctor and his specialized knowledge and training."

"Yeah," I said, "but one doctor used to be enough. Today you'll be referred to three or four different specialists before you're told what's wrong with you."

"What's wrong with you is that you should have lived in the 1800's."

"Sometimes I think so too. These days you'd be ill-advised even to sign your name without consulting a lawyer. That specialization costs money."

"Sometimes it's better to pay the specialist to make sure things are done right," she said. "Remember when you tried to rewire the house?"

"Stop complaining about the blinking lights," I said. "Okay, I give up. See if you can get any cell phone reception. I think we're going to need Mike to tow this thing."

"I thought it was just running a little rough?" she asked.

"It was. But now I have leftover parts."

I can understand why certain occupations have become so specialized. But I don't understand why it has to happen to my hobbies too. Look at hunting and fishing, for instance.

It used to be that you put on old clothes to go fishing and added a wool jacket to go hunting. Now you need a specialized wardrobe of very expensive clothing featuring terrain-specific camo patterns, made of water-proof, breathable, scent-trapping, sound-deadening, high-loft, moisture-wicking, space-age fabric.

It used to be that you carried the same old familiar shotgun with a selection of shells for whatever you hunted. Now, whether you're after turkeys, ducks, grouse or deer, you're told you need a shotgun specific to the task.

Imagine what would happen if you had to depend on a network of specialists just to go hunting for the weekend.

"Where's your truck," my brother Gary asked.

190

"I rented this specialty vehicle from Wilderness Wheels," I said. "It's more appropriate for this weekend's hunt. I'm disappointed, though. It's running a little rough."

"We can tweak it a little when we get there," he said. "Did you get the scouting reports from Here for Deer?"

"Naturally," I said. "They sent in a specialist to analyze the deer herd. We've got the maps from Aerial for Antlers that detail the feeding and bedding areas and the best stand locations. Their infrared scan showed lots of small game too, but we're specializing in deer this weekend."

When we got to camp my brother was furious.

"We should have set up camp ourselves," he said. "I specifically told Tons of Tents that I like to sleep with my head toward the door, slightly elevated."

"Well, they're the experts," I said. "I wouldn't complain. The guys in the tent-riggers union can get pretty ugly if you upset them."

The scouts had been correct. It was a fabulous place to hunt. But I missed a chance at a trophy buck because I didn't react in time.

"Hello, Tracks and Racks? I've crossed some fresh sign. Okay, I'll hold," I said. When their specialist came to the phone, I filled him in on the measurements of the tracks, droppings, scrapes and rubs I'd located.

"So in your expert opinion, this buck is worth pursuing, correct?" I asked. "That's all I wanted to know. Yes, just a moment. I'll get you my credit card number."

After an intense hunt, I spotted the buck. I quickly grabbed my cell phone and punched in the number for Game Gaugers Limited.

"Yes, I believe this might be trophy class. Stand by; I'll transmit the digital image. Well, according to the laser range-finder, it's 107 yards away, slightly downhill, negligible wind."

"So in your expert opinion this is a keeper? Excellent!

191

What? You can fly in a marksman from Surrogate Shooters?
Half an hour by chopper, you say? No, I don't think so. I
want to take this buck all by myself. You can patch me
through to your Better Ballistics department, though. I want
to double check the trajectory."

Just as I was ready for the shot, the deer bolted. My
brother had better luck and shot a modest six-pointer.

"I just hope Venison Video gets here before Backwoods
Butchers arrives to field-dress and drag it away," he said. "I
phoned in the GPS coordinates 45 minutes ago. They ought
to be here by now."

"This is their busy season," I said. "Why don't we head
back? Kampfire Kitchens should be rolling in with our supper
and I'm starving."

"That's the one thing you've always specialized in," Gary
said. "Second helpings."

Being Flexible

(Originally published by Game & Fish Publications, April 2004)

My first three kids are well past the official age of taking anything I say seriously. My fourth is still at the young age where anything I say is funny.

Sometime in between, there is about a six-month window when the warm breeze of fatherly wisdom can flow into their impressionable minds. Before and after that moment, the window is locked, the blinds are closed, the curtains are drawn and the security system is activated. Only a chilly draft of pop music and cable television can filter through.

"You have to adapt to what's happening on the water," I tried to explain to them anyway. "If the fly rod and streamer aren't working, switch rods and try a spinner or go to the traditional worm kabob. Live minnows can be very effective.

"You have to be flexible if you're going to be successful on this trout stream," I continued. "A fishing rod is flexible. It bends, but doesn't break, whether you have a big fish on or if you're just snagged. Line, on the other hand, will stretch only so far. Then it just snaps. In fishing and in life, be the rod. Don't be the line."

The kids just laughed.

"Oh brother," my wife Dawn said from behind the magazine she was reading. "Why don't you just 'be the dad' and give them money so they can get ice cream?"

That gave me an idea: bribery. I'd try bribery.

"Okay, kids, here's the deal. We'll fish for another half

hour, then we'll get ice cream for us and a diet soda for Mom."

"Tick, tick, tick," Sean said. "While you guys are 'being the rods,' I'll 'be the clock,' so we don't stay here too long."

"I'm still 'being the rod,'" said Stephanie, the youngest. She stood at attention, then suddenly started jerking her body and hopping around. "Look, I've got a fish. I've got a fish. Quickly, Brian, 'be the net.'"

"Mom's 'being the net,'" Brian said. "Don't you remember Dad told us that after Mom landed him, there was only one way out?"

"Yeah," Matt said. "Dad was 'being the fish' when Mom hooked him and his only way out was suffocating death."

"I never said that," I said. I could feel Dawn's laser beam eyes burning through the pages of the magazine. Soon her temper would be ignited. "I definitely never said anything like that. Now let's get back to fishing."

"Look, Stephanie," I said. "This is how I want you to cast." Naturally, it did not go as expected.

"How can I catch a fish with the hook way up there in that tree?" she said.

Five minutes later I was stuck upside down on a thin branch over-hanging the stream.

"You've almost got it Dad," Sean said.

"Yeah, 'be the tree' and branch out," Brian said, obviously giddy at my predicament.

"Dawn!" I yelled. "Do something!"

She had finally put the magazine down.

"Suffocating death?" she said. "Maybe I'll do something. Maybe I'll go get a 'diet soda'."

"Look, Dad, the branch is 'being the rod,'" Stephanie said. "See how flexible it is?"

The branch's flexibility had its limits and one slightly overweight middle-aged man was beyond them. The branch and I ended up in the stream, which was "being a stream" and nothing else, with typically cold, fast-moving water.

"Be the bobber, Dad, don't be the sinker," Matt said.

"D-Dawn, I, I was only kid-id-ding before." I was shivering uncontrollably the instant I hit the water. "B-but now, now, I, I'm not kid-id-ing. Pl-please he-help m-me out."

Dawn tossed my fishing rod out to me. The other end of the line was still attached to the tree.

"Here," she said. "Reel yourself in."

The line held, but the rod not only bent, it broke. Still, I was able to claw my way out of the stream. I stood there, soaking wet and freezing.

"Now can we have ice cream?" Stephanie asked. My lack of a reply was her answer.

I went to the car to see if there was a towel or any dry clothes. Dawn went back to reading her magazine. Her hands clutched it so tightly that her fingernails were tearing the cover. Yup, she was still mad. The boys, realizing by experience that it would be some time before there would be a cessation of hostilities, decided to look for their fun elsewhere and went back to fishing on their own.

I found an old blanket in the trunk of the car. We usually used it to cover the back seat at times when we brought our dogs along on a hike. It was covered with little muddy doggy footprints and little doggy hair. But I was flexible. When there are no alternatives, you have to be. I wrapped myself in the blanket.

Two hours later, Stephanie was standing next to me as I made mock casts with my new rod near the water. She finally had her ice cream – chocolate with chunks of candy in it and sprinkles on top. It was all over her face and dripping down the cone and along her wrist.

"You like to fish a lot, don't you, Dad?" she asked.

"Yes, I do."

"Your shoes are still squeaking water out of them," she said. "That's funny."

I nodded.

"You still smell like our wet dogs," she said. "That's funny too."

I nodded again.

"Mom said it was very flexible of you to take us here to the shopping mall," she said. "But I don't think there are any fish in this fountain. There are lots of pennies in there, though. Can you catch some of them?"

"I may need every one of them and more by the time Mom's done shopping here."

"Brothers went to see some kill-'em movie that wasn't 'propriate for me, so I got ice cream. Mom said she was going to buy a whole new wardrobe. What's a wardrobe?"

"Clothes mostly," I said. "And probably several new pairs of shoes."

"When I grow up I hope my husband will be flexible just like you, Dad," she said.

The Barlow Family
Reunion

(Originally published by Game & Fish Publications, June 2004)

Family reunions have long been part of our hunting and fishing heritage. In fact, it was the early frontiersman who popularized them.

First understand that the basic unit of related people is the immediate family, so-named for its constant sense of urgency in going about its daily activities. My own family is immersed in the immediate:

"Dad, I need that money Mom promised me right now," said son Matt.

"Dad, I'm late for work and my car's almost out of gas. I'm taking your truck, okay? Bye," said son Brian.

"Dad, remember you have to take me to soccer practice," said son Sean. "We should be leaving now."

"Dad, the canoe's in the back of the truck," said Brian. "Do you want to take it out before I leave? It's going to be busy today at Chuck's Chunky Chicken and I'm late already."

"I was going to go fishing in a little while," I said.

"You said you were going to take me to get a Folly Dolly Playhouse today," said daughter Stephanie. "I really need it now."

"How can you go fishing?" wife Dawn asked. "You promised to pick up the new shrubs at the garden shop today."

"I'll get to that in a minute," I said. "Then I was going

fishing. It's my only day off."

"In a minute means never," Dawn said. "I'll do it myself like I do everything else. When do I ever get a day off?"

Dawn then got the immediate family moving immediately.

"Brian, here's money for gas. It'll be quicker for you to stop and fill your own car than it would be to unload Dad's truck," she said. "Matt here's the money I promised you."

"Hey that's my wallet," I said.

"Matt, help Dad take the canoe off the back of the truck," she said. "Sean, Stephanie, get into the truck. We'll drop Sean off at soccer and look for Stephanie's doll house on the way to the garden shop."

Two minutes later the immediate family was gone and I was left standing alone next to my canoe on the front lawn.

It was no different in the pioneer days. There were always immediate tasks that had to be done for the immediate family before the man of the house could go hunting and fishing.

That's why many brave outdoorsmen gave up the certainty of hearty, home-cooked meals of cornbread smothered with squirrel chunks and gravy, and ventured to the frontier where there was only the hope of fried trout and broiled venison steaks.

I say these outdoorsmen were brave, not because they had to survive the dangers of the wilderness, but because they actually had the nerve to return home after extended expeditions of a year or two.

"Darling, you're home just in time. I have a list of things you must do right away," the pioneer wife Dawn might have said. "Children this is your father. I'll throw some squirrel chunks and gravy in the kettle because I remember it's your favorite and also because since you've been gone we haven't had anything else to eat."

That's how our rich tradition of the family reunion began. Many outdoorsmen today still have family reunions every year or two. But it's much harder to get away from the

198

immediate family and go on extended hunting and fishing expeditions because the wife is sure to come after you for failure to pay child support.

So, modern day reunions often involve the extended family. The extended family consists of a series of immediate families all related to each other, but who don't necessarily like each other. Immediate families rarely have time to interact with their extended families except through intermittent Christmas cards and at funerals.

With the extended family, as the name suggests, you're obligated to extend invitations to distant relatives when there is any milestone event within your immediate family, such as a wedding or graduation.

This extending of invitations is important so that those distant relatives won't speak ill of your immediate family to other distant relatives.

"That Steve never amounted to much, you know. All he does is write about hunting and fishing. And those kids are undisciplined brats. They brought a dead raccoon into the house the last time I was there. I feel sorry for Dawn."

In our extended family, the responsibility of planning and hosting the sometimes annual family reunion rotates from one immediate family to the next. The last time it was our turn to host, Dawn looked over our Christmas card list of relatives so we wouldn't forget to invite anyone.

"What if we invite your family and mine?" I suggested.

"Sure," Dawn said. "Or why don't we just re-enact the bloodiest battle of the Civil War instead?"

"You're right," I said. "Bad idea. What if we have the reunion at the lake. We'll start out with some trap shooting at the rod and gun club, then have a little fishing derby for the kids beyond the beach, past the picnic area."

So with a certain pioneering spirit, we ventured into our first ever shooting and fishing family reunion. Here are some of the highlights:

Aunt Molly and Uncle Carl broke the most clay pigeons in the husband and wife category at the family reunion, not surprising since they always broke the most dishes in the family fight category as well.

"Congratulations Aunt Molly. Good shooting Uncle Carl," I said. "You remember Uncle Carl don't you Dawn?"

"You should remember Uncle Carl and I were divorced eight years ago," said Aunt Molly. "This is your Uncle Bob."

"Do you still have that Christmas card list," I asked Dawn the moment we were alone. "We'd better scratch out Uncle Carl and pencil in Uncle Bob."

Grandpa Luke wasn't my grandfather, but since he was in his 80's, the grumpy old griper was probably grandfather to some unfortunate relative. I think he was my great uncle three times removed. He was removed at least that many times from the family reunion because no one could put up with his constant complaining for very long.

He kept motoring his electric wheelchair into positions where he could maximize his misery on us all.

"Push me to the shooting line," he snapped. "The darn battery in this chair is just about dead."

He'd broken 15 straight pigeons when the trap machine broke and we had to launch the rest with a hand thrower.

"Come on, come on," he complained. "I could be dead before I finish my round. No, not like that. Get some loft into the thing."

Then, mysteriously and most likely by general agreement, the brake was released on Luke's wheelchair and he rolled backwards toward the lake, his ranting and raving gradually fading from earshot.

At the lake, the kids were busy tangling line, pulling apart worms, and wading along the shore after bullfrogs. Some threw stones in an impromptu distance contest, with extra style points given to the biggest splashes.

Cousin Bridget, engaged in non-stop gossip with Aunt

Madge, reached blindly into her ice chest and shrieked like a dying rabbit predator call when she came up with a wiggling sunfish in the palm of her hand.

Uncle Jack presided over the barbecue grill, and just smiled when two more still-flopping sunfish appeared through the smoke on the grill. He turned them with his spatula. His wife, Aunt Elsie was upset with him for showing off when he later ate them with a sprinkle of lemon juice.

When the day was through, vague, obligatory invitations were extended to all the relatives in the "we must get together like this more often" tradition.

Then each immediate family packed up and headed home, adequately informed about the latest family business, and content, just as the early frontiersmen had been, that the family reunion was only a sometimes annual event.

Deer Parties
vs. Going Solo

(Originally published by Game & Fish Publications, November 2002)

Certain things you just shouldn't do alone. Celebrating your birthday, fixing leaky plumbing, and playing baseball are all things best done with other people. Actually, fixing leaky plumbing is best done "by" other people, not "with" other people, but you get the idea.

Deer hunting is something you can enjoy by yourself, with one or two companions, or with a whole cast of characters. A group of deer is known as a herd. But a group of deer hunters is known appropriately as a hunting party. The more hunters, the more wild the party and the less hunting get done.

Sometimes, members of a hunting party wander off in separate directions for the day's hunt. Some sort of rudimentary organization is helpful to prevent the hunters from blundering into each other all day long. Otherwise, imagine the conversation back at camp.

"It'll be dark in a few minutes. Barlow's not back yet?"

"I saw him down at the edge of the marsh at about nine this morning, emptying the water out of his boots."

"I saw him too, at about 10:30. He had just finished his lunch and he wanted to know if I had any extra sandwiches he could have."

"I saw him at about 1:15 half way up Win acre Ridge. But he didn't see me. He was sound asleep with his jacket pulled up over his head. I think he was still breathing."

"He must have been, because at about three he came skipping across the meadow I was watching from the edge of the hardwoods. He looked like he was trying to catch butterflies."

"We'll give him until morning before we call search and rescue again. What's for dinner?"

Sometimes some control freak in the group will insist that the hunting party get extremely organized and put on a deer drive. I normally volunteer to provide this service for my hunting parties.

Simply, a deer drive is where some unlucky members of the party have to push, claw, stomp, and crawl through the most tangled, overgrown vegetation in the hopes of scaring deer out into the open, where other, more fortunate members of the party, are lounging in strategic locations behind trees or logs, waiting to ambush them.

Deer drives normally take about three hours to execute properly. The first two hours are spent hashing out the game plan and assigning positions to hunters.

"Mike, you take a stand over by the lightning-split maple. Know the one I mean?" I said.

Mike nodded vaguely.

"Dave and Gary, I want you about 50 yards apart at the south end of the pines, where you can see anything that comes through that way. Stu and Wayne, hunker down in the general vicinity of the large boulder at the top of the draw. The rest of us will push through the thick stuff."

As the hunters head off to their posts, typically everyone is charged with anticipation.

"I don't care. Whatever you say."

"This will never work."

"What a waste of time."

"Don't argue with him. Let's just get it over with."

The next 15 minutes are spent putting on the drive. The last 45 minutes are spent trying to get everyone to meet up in the same location -- no small feat -- to analyze why no one saw a single deer and to plot the activities for the rest of the day.

"Where is he now? Has anyone seen him?"

"He's probably chasing butterflies again."

Going solo is a completely different experience. Whether the hunt lasts several hours or several days, the challenges of going solo attract primarily the daring adventurer, independent and confident. He enjoys the solitude. He distills life to its basics, to hunter and prey. He likes things simple.

"There's no one as simple as you, dear," my wife Dawn commented as I packed for yet another solo trek. "When are you going to admit that none of those loafers you call friends really wants to hunt with you?"

"Ridiculous," I said. "They're all just very busy. Besides, if they hunted without me, who would organize their deer drives?"

Normally when I hunt alone, I start out sitting in a likely spot. A likely spot is one where I am concealed, warm, dry and comfortable, with a view that conjures in my imagination the hope that a deer might walk through.

Hope is the great essential for sitting for any length of time. Lose hope and a likely spot becomes exposed, cold, damp, and uncomfortable. Normally this occurs after a half an hour or until the food in my day pack is gone.

That's the time for the solo hunter to get the circulation flowing again and to start wandering about. If I catch a glimpse of a deer and it's moving out of range, I normally put on one of my patented one-man deer drives.

In a one-man drive, I only rarely spend two hours arguing with myself about strategy, although I have been known to close my eyes briefly to contemplate my course of action. First I lighten my load -- I take off my day pack and other gear that might slow me down. Then, after I hack my way through the impenetrable jungle, I suddenly sprint out in a wide loop to come out ahead of any deer I might have spooked.

Several times this has worked and deer have walked right up to me. If just once I could remember not to set my gun down alongside my day pack when I start my drive, I might get a shot.

As long as you aren't reckless, hunting alone is relatively safe. Breaking a leg or falling on your head and dying a slow, painful death alone miles from home is actually preferable to doing more embarrassing things in front of a large hunting party.

Getting caught napping or chasing butterflies are two things that come to mind. No one will believe you were planning and executing a one-man deer drive.

Santa And The
Merry Christmyths

(Originally published by Game & Fish Publications, December 1991)

There have been many myths perpetuated over the years about a hunting acquaintance of mine, Santa Claus, and I'm glad to have this opportunity to set the record straight.

I met Santa one December about twelve years back while grouse hunting. I was nestled all too snugly in a particularly nasty patch of brush, succeeding at tearing the final shreds of cloth from my new hunting jacket.

I clawed my way through the prickers to a small clearing. Then what to my wondering eyes should appear, but Santa, sitting on a stump, an ancient side-by-side shotgun over his knee.

The jolly old elf, so lively and quick, had just completed a double -- he had flushed two partridges from a pear tree -- and had stopped to catch his breath and savor the moment.

I wasn't sure who he was at first. I mean, you're used to seeing him in shopping malls, not in the middle of some pricker patch, right?

He looked me up and down. Finally, he said, "I suppose you're going to ask me for a new hunting jacket again this Christmas?"

"Santa, it is you! You know, I thought you looked familiar. The white beard, the dimples how merry, the belly that shakes like a bowl full of jelly, they're all there. I guess the blaze orange suit was what threw me. What happened to your red

one?"

"I change from time to time. You ought to try it," he said. "And would you mind getting off of my lap?"

Myth number one exposed. Santa doesn't always wear the same red suit. He explained that he had tried the traditional red hunter's plaid, but Mrs. Claus, being a bit near-sighted, had trouble picking him out of the crowd at the elves' annual gun show and flea market.

He said he'd tried stripes once, but a policeman stopped him one Christmas Eve as he was coming out of someone's chimney, his sack over his shoulder.

He had some fast explaining to do. If he hadn't been able to describe the fly rod he'd delivered to the policeman's house the year before, Santa might have spent Christmas in the pokey.

He had just finished telling me this when an old, pink-nosed English setter came trotting out of the brush and dropped the second bird at Santa's feet.

"Good boy, Rudolph," Santa said as he patted the dog on the head. Myth number two exposed: Rudolph is not a reindeer. I was dumbfounded.

I soon learned other things about Santa. For instance, he didn't always operate his now famous holiday gift delivery service.

As a young elf he was a loner and moved around quite a bit. In those days, it's sad to say, society didn't always extend equal rights to short, fat citizens with pointy ears. Now, thanks to Santa, such citizens can even become columnists for outdoor magazines.

He did some trapping and ran a now-defunct guide service in the northern states where he designed his famous red parka and built quite a reputation as a cold weather person.

Myth number three exposed: Santa does not live at the North Pole. Because of his celebrity status, Santa would be constantly hounded by well-wishers and greedy gift-seekers if his true residence were known.

"Let me just say that my 4x4 pickup used less than a half of a tank of gas to get me bird hunting today," he said.

"No sleigh?" I asked, mentally noting exposed myth number four.

"No snow," he pointed out.

Santa's love of the outdoors soon led him to become active in many game management and habitat restoration causes. His involvement in these conservation efforts added to his reputation as a true friend to the reindeer and other animals.

Santa was a successful hunter and, during the lean years, was always generous enough to stop by the houses of the poor to help out with a rabbit, pheasant or whatever was in season.

Santa soon became a clearinghouse for other charitable organizations, mostly sporting goods manufacturers, who donated shotguns, hunting knives and fishing tackle. In this way Santa could promote his conservation ideals while giving people an economical form of recreation and helping them to provide for themselves.

Most of the charities wanted Santa to deliver the gifts on Christmas, but Santa was reluctant at first. It made no sense. The end of December was no time to promote sporting goods and outdoor living. For the most part it was too late for hunting and too early for fishing.

In the end Santa conceded and delivered his sporting goods on Christmas. After all, Christmas was the season of love, hope and generosity. Those ideals, he considered, were not inconsistent with his notion of a balanced, loving relationship with nature, a nurturing of the environment in return for the bounty it provided. Santa started decorating evergreen trees to promote these beliefs.

From there, well, you can guess the rest of the story. Through the generations the legend of Santa Claus became distorted, especially by city dwellers who had lost touch with the land.

Just to stay in business, Santa had to deliver other types of gifts to appease those who spent their entire lives walking on concrete and blacktop, never to know the thrill of hunting birds in pricker patches.

"I've always wondered, Santa," I said. "How do you deliver so many wool socks and miracle hook sharpeners to so many hunters and fishermen without getting mixed up?"

"Over the years I've had to rely on those other benevolent gift-givers: the wives. Yours is especially nice. You know that new shotgun you've been wanting for so long?"

"You mean my wife is going to get it for me?"

Santa just winked. He obviously didn't want to spoil the surprise.

"Here then, Santa," I said. "Take my old shotgun and give it to some needy hunter. I insist."

I walked him down to his pickup truck, handed him my shotgun and the twenty dollars he said he'd need for shipping and handling.

That's the last I saw of Santa. But I heard him exclaim as he drove out of sight, "I'm not really Santa Claus you gullible nitwit."

(That Santa, what a kidder.)

Myth number five exposed: Old bearded men you meet in the woods are seldom Santa Claus.

Fishing-In-Law

Mothers-in-law are like largemouth bass. They cause quite a commotion on the surface, and down deep they hang on tirelessly as they attempt to pull you down to their level.

A man needs to understand at the time of his marriage that the mother-in-law is part of the bargain. It's a package deal. And when your wife and mother-in-law get together, it's like getting a sore throat along with a stuffy nose – the two can gang up on you and make you miserable.

There's no better time to go fishing than when your mother-in-law comes to visit. Unfortunately for me, the last time my mother-in-law came to town, the kids were in school and my wife, Dawn, had to work. That left me as chairman of the entertainment committee.

"But it's my only real day off," I said. "I was going to go fishing."

"She doesn't come up that often," Dawn said. "You can go fishing any time. Or you can ask her to go with you. She used to love to go fishing when she was a young girl."

"I don't believe your mother ever was a young girl," I said.

"It would give you two a chance to get to know each other," she said.

"You and I have been married for 21 years. Your mother and I know each other all too well. That's the problem. She doesn't like me."

When my mother-in-law arrived, we exchanged the usual pleasantries.

"It's good to see you again Grandma Betty. You're looking

211

well," I said.

"Look at you," she laughed. "Lost a little hair and put on a little weight since I was up last? Time to trade him in on a new one, Dawn."

"Steve was going fishing, Mom," Dawn said, "and…"

"Oh that's all right," she said. "I can just sit here alone and watch television like I do at home. I'm a little tired anyway after traveling more than a thousand miles just to visit with you two."

Dawn gave me a piercing look so I wouldn't miss my queue.

"Hey, I've got an idea," I said. "Why don't you come with me? I'm just going to paddle around Little Stump Lake for a while. You might enjoy that."

My hopes of fishing were shattered like a clay pigeon at the Sunday trap league when Grandma Betty said, "Okay."

Normally my favorite place in a canoe is in the rear. When I sit in the front, there's nothing ahead of me except open water and I always get the uneasy feeling, based on experience, that I'm going to fall in head first.

Seated in the back, I have the whole canoe in front of me. Also, I can stop paddling any time I get tired without the paddler in the front being immediately aware of it, so I get a free ride. It's also difficult at times to hear what the person in the front is saying, which I figured would be perfect when canoeing with Grandma Betty.

What I hadn't anticipated was that Grandma Betty would insist on helping to paddle. She sent a shower of murky lake water into my face each time she stabbed or slapped at the water with her paddle. I was soaked before we were 50 feet from shore.

"This is fun," she said with a cackle. Although she never looked back, I was certain she knew exactly what she was doing.

I tried to weigh the pleasure I'd get from intentionally

tipping the canoe over against the possible loss of my fishing tackle. I decided for the moment to bide my time.

I stopped paddling and we glided into a likely spot. I began to rig my line with a topwater plug.

"Do you mind if I try one of those speckled plastic worms?" Grandma Betty asked. I had no idea she actually intended to fish. I hadn't brought an extra rod, so I was forced to relinquish mine.

She swung the rod like she was stretching to swat flies on the ceiling. She lurched one way and I defensively dove another to avoid getting speared in the face with her hook on her backcast. The canoe rocked violently.

"I think I've got one!" she shouted. "Get the net, get the net, get the net! What are you doing back there? Get the net!"

"Easy Grandma," I said. "You'll fry your pacemaker. You're probably just snagged."

Her 18-inch bass splashed to the surface as soon as the words were out of my mouth. Moments later, Grandma Betty posed for a photo with her first fish in fifty years.

"I'm one up on you," she said.

"Today, maybe," I said. "Overall I think we're even. I caught a fish once too. I've just been in a little slump the last 30 years or so."

Grandma Betty directed me as I paddled around the lake the rest of the day. She fished and I dodged her backcasts. She caught fish and posed for more photos. I paddled some more.

We went out of our way a couple of times – once to visit some ducks and once to try to sneak up on a turtle that was sunning itself on a log jutting out of the water. She helped to paddle then, and I was grateful for the water in my face.

"What the heck," I thought to myself. "She's having a good time, and it's not like I would have caught anything anyway. Dawn will be happy. That good will should be worth about three more unopposed fishing outings over the next month before it wears off and I'll have to do another good deed."

Back on land, Grandma Betty decided to try her luck from shore while I bent over to haul the canoe out of the water. I had been agile enough all day to avoid her casts. But I didn't see this one coming and she hooked me deep in my back pocket.

"I think I've got another one!" she shouted. "Get the net, get the net, get the net!"

"Forget the net, forget the net, forget the net!" I shouted. "Get the long-nose pliers!"

After some emergency shore-side surgery, Grandma Betty style, it was Grandma Betty who drove us home. On the way, I tried to keep my wound elevated, which meant pretty much sticking it out of the window.

"Did you two have a good time?" Dawn asked when we got home.

"Well, I've got to admit," Grandma Betty said with a smile. "I got to see a side of your husband I've never seen before."

Just Tagging Along

(Originally published by Game & Fish Publications, March 2004)

Just tagging along on someone's hunting or fishing trip is like just tagging along on someone's honeymoon. Someone is bound to feel crowded and someone else is bound to feel left out.

My wife, Dawn, said she felt like she was just tagging along on our honeymoon. I don't think she would have said that if the fish had been biting and the tent hadn't leaked. Somehow, sending her a postcard that read, "Wish you were here," wouldn't have been the same if she hadn't just tagged along.

I have been the tagger – the one tagging along -- and the taggee – the one someone tags along with -- on enough outings to know there are unwritten guidelines governing each person's responsibilities.

I had to learn that the hard way. I tagged along on a hunting trip with three guys from work a few years ago. We were sitting around the campfire discussing the strategy for the next morning's hunt when I made the mistake of putting in my two cents worth.

"After you guys invited me along, I went out and bought a map of the area," I said, anxious to help. "I marked some areas where I think the deer will naturally funnel through. If we put a guy over here, for instance…"

Glenn grabbed me by the arm and pulled me aside.

"What are you doing?" he whispered. "You're just

215

tagging along, remember? We come here every year. We're the starting team. You're just subbing off the bench for the visiting squad. We're calling the plays in the huddle. If the guys think you're trying to play quarterback, they may not invite you next time."

"I'm sorry, Glenn," I said. "I'll just sit back and be a spectator."

As the years went by I eventually became a member of the team. It then became my job to be wary of others who wanted to just tag along.

"So, Dave and you are going fishing up at Spruce Pond?" Les asked.

At this point Les was obeying dutifully the first rule of someone who just tags along: he was refraining from actually coming out and inviting himself along. He had spotted me picking up some last minute supplies at Vern's Fishing Tackle Emporium. He knew I had something planned.

"You're going to camp there the whole weekend?" he asked. Les was not only on a fact-finding mission, he was fishing for an invitation.

"Yes," I replied, hoping my one-word response would not be construed as opening a door of opportunity. But it was one word too many. Les had succeeded in engaging me in conversation. He had won the first volley.

"Gee, I haven't been fishing at Spruce Pond in 20 years," Les said. "There were plenty of times I wanted to go, but business was good at the time and the kids were young. You know how it is. Of course, I have more time than I can stand since Irma ran off with that vacuum cleaner salesman. I'm practically stir crazy around the house on weekends."

Les was performing the classic "woe-is-me" routine known to all who just tag along. It was a predictable strategy, but no less difficult to defend against. He had made it clear too that he was available to tag along if by chance I did invite him.

"Why don't you tag along with us?" I offered strictly out of obligation. All was not lost yet. The second rule of those who just tag along states that you can never accept the first invitation offered since it is an invitation of courtesy and not sincerity.

"Oh you guys don't need me slowing you down," he said. "I'm not even sure I could find my old sleeping bag. Still, if you aren't leaving until Friday evening, I could probably pull my gear together. How do you guys work the meals? Do you have a designated cook or does each guy fend for himself? What kind of tackle should I bring? Are the fish hitting anything in particular this time of year?"

Les was tricky. He was talking gear, food and other logistics as if he had already received the all-important confirmation of a second invitation. It would have been difficult to say, "Nice talking to you, Les. See you around," and just walk away.

"Are you guys riding up together or are you going to meet up there?" Les asked. "My truck's running a little rough."

"I'll probably have room in my truck," I conceded.

Les had played it like a pro. In one fell swoop, he had finagled from me a second invitation and a ride. That wasn't the end of it. Les used his "just-tagging-along" status for "guest-of-honor" treatment the whole weekend.

We stopped at a diner on the way to Spruce Pond that Friday.

"Since, I'm just tagging along," Les said, "I didn't realize the plan was to stop for supper. I didn't bring much money."

"No problem, Les," I said. "We'll spot you this time."

During that outing, Les didn't tote any firewood, clean up after meals, row a single stroke or help to clean the fish. He not only "just tagged along," but he tagged the other guys for their best lures, spare line, and new chest waders when his were torn.

Near the end of the weekend, one of the guys mentioned

217

coming up again in a couple of weeks. I cringed, sure that Les would start positioning himself for another invitation.

"I'd like to come," Les said, pre-empting any excuses we were preparing. "But my brother gave me a couple of tickets to the baseball game that Saturday afternoon."

"Really?" I said. "Is that the same brother who has season tickets along the first base line every season? Gee, I haven't been to a game in years."

One hour later, Les slipped and uttered a first, then second invitation. If I worked it right, I was confident I could get him to drive to the ballpark and spring for the hot dogs.